MATT NEWTON
The No B.S. Guide to the Acting Biz

Matt Newton is an acclaimed on-camera acting coach, the founder of the prestigious MN Acting Studio in New York City and Connecticut, an industry expert contributor to *Backstage*, award-winning filmmaker, and on-set coach for Ava Duvernay's Emmy-winning *When They See Us*, *Jessica Jones, Orange Is the New Black, Blue Bloods, Master of None* and *The Affair*. Newton teaches acting workshops all over the world and has coached both Emmy Award winners and Golden Globe nominees.

As an actor, Newton has guest-starred on dozens of TV shows, including *Gilmore Girls, Ugly Betty, Drake and Josh Go Hollywood, The Americans, Royal Pains, All My Children, Guiding Light, Strangers with Candy, Dragnet*, as well as the films *Van Wilder* (with Ryan Reynolds), *Men Who Stare at Goats* (with Jeff Bridges), *Poster Boy*, and *Dahmer* (with Jeremy Renner).

As a filmmaker, Matt has written and directed the short films *Hide/Seek, Pretty People Inc, Sins of the Son*, and *Vacation Rental*, for which he won Best Director at the Northeast Film Festival.

Newton earned a degree in Drama from Vassar College and continued his undergraduate education at the highly regarded National Theatre Institute in Waterford, CT (where he is also on the faculty).

www.MattCNewton.com

ALSO BY MATT NEWTON
10 Steps to Breaking into Acting

The No B.S. Guide to the Acting Biz

By Matt Newton

Table of Contents

Acknowledgments i

Foreword.. ii

Covid Update.. vi

Introduction viii

Chapter 1: Video Killed the Radio Star.................................... 1
The TV, Film and Theatre Market

Chapter 2: Bite and Smile... 5
Commercials: Union vs. Non-Union

Chapter 3: Hit Your Mark, Say Your Lines and Don't Be Weird............... 8
What it's Really Like on Set

Chapter 4: Auditioning for Dummies 14
The Casting Process

Chapter 5: When in Doubt, Zoom in 20
Auditioning in Your Underwear

Chapter 6: Hot Mess Vibes 25
On Dealing with Nerves and Confidence

Chapter 7: Cue Cards and Cry Sticks 28
The ABC's of Self-Taping

Chapter 8: The Art of the Deal 36
Agents and Managers

Chapter 9: No Pay, No Meal, No Credit, No Fun...................... 41
Your Demo Reel Footage

Chapter 10: Speed Dating... 44
Pay-to-Meet Workshops

Chapter 11: I Play Psychopaths 48
Your Actor "Type"

Chapter 12: Hit Me Up on Insta... 50
The Importance of Social Media

Chapter 13: Get Off Your Ass 53
 A Guide to Creating Your Own Work

Chapter 14: Brand Spanking New 65
 Advice for Newbies Young and Old

Chapter 15: Stage Moms, Inc. 68
 Advice for Kids and Parents

Chapter 16: Reality Check 75
 Hard Core Truths About Being a Professional Actor

Chapter 17: Interview with a TV/Film Casting Director 79
 Stephanie Holbrook

Chapter 18: Interview with a Theatrical Talent Agent 87
 Robert Attermann from A3 Artists Agency

Chapter 19: Interview with a Youth Talent Manager 92
 Peggy Becker from Parkside Talent

Chapter 20: Conversation with an Editor 98
 Howard Leder from NBC's "This is Us"

Chapter 21: Stories from the Trenches 104
 Audition Horror Stories from Working Actors

In Closing: #pleasedontsuck 113
 The Business of You

APPENDIX 115

Acknowledgments

Thanks to all of my talented students at MN Acting Studio who inspired me to write this book, who continue to ask the tough questions, and who deserve the world. I wish I could hand it to you. Thanks to my incredible teachers and friends Karen, Jordyn, Dena, Amy, Bryan, Van, and Mila. Your combination of expertise, patience, and inspiration is a force to be reckoned with. Thanks to Robert, Stephanie, Beth, Paul, Howard and Peggy for supporting this vision of educating the masses and giving your wonderful perspectives from your decades of experience. Thanks to my talented student, friend and editor Stacey Van Gorder Leung for her tireless dedication in helping me make sense of this mess. Finally, thanks to my wife Liana, and my beautiful kids James and Frances for allowing me special "Daddy time" to write this. I will be home soon to play with the trains, I promise. Right now, it's go time.

Foreword
By Michael Urie

The summer after I graduated from high school, I took my very first trip to New York City with a theater group from the Texas community college where I was about to start my higher education. We saw thirteen shows in ten days. I was, as we say in Texas, "a pig in shit." I still occasionally smell hot summer garbage in Times Square and smile, reminded of my first time there. A few months earlier I had changed my mind about what I wanted to pursue after graduation. I'd known I wanted to work in the theater for all of high school and, convinced I didn't have the talent to be competitive as an actor in show business, I set my sights on the only professionals in the theater I knew personally: drama teachers. My teachers were my idols. They were doing what I wanted to do: making plays. In the final months of high school, thanks to a few of the plays we put up and some of the acting competitions I participated in (in Texas everything is a contest), I started to think I might just have what it takes. It was a moment during a poetry reading contest that changed everything. I thought I was reading a dramatic poem, the height of teenage angst, rage and fear and sorrow... But the audience laughed. Not AT me, but with me. They thought I was funny and they liked it. And I liked it. So I leaned in...I pinpointed what they found funny and I kept doing it...And they loved it and I won the contest. This was my first yes. Yes, to being entirely me.

But, wait, cut back to the New York trip, the thirteen shows and the hot garbage. After a very exciting tour of The Juilliard School, my soon to be college drama professor/NY trip chaperone took me aside and asked me if I was going to audition for Juilliard. I thought I might. He paused and said more directly, "No, are you going to audition?" I said, "yes, definitely." He said, "This place has your name written all over it." I agreed to audition because he told me to, but I still didn't think I had a snowball's chance. One year later, I was moving to New York to attend Juilliard.

ii

Now, I realize I didn't get into Juilliard simply because I said "yes" to auditioning. But if I hadn't said yes...

Saying yes has been instrumental to my decision-making process ever since.

When you're breaking into the business (which, by the way, is not a science), everyone will have an opinion because everyone has their own unique experience. Our own experience is all we have to navigate because the way in which your career unfolds is unlike any other. The best experiences I've had, the biggest breaks, the greatest artistic achievements, are all thanks to a "yes."

My agent and manager urged me to pass on my biggest break, *Ugly Betty*. But I said yes to the audition anyway, not because I had some premonition it would be a hit television show, but because it was a job that I thought I could book. Based on the people involved, the material, and the description of the character, I had a hunch it would spark - and I was right. It was the single most important job of my career. It's also where I met the author of this book, Matt Newton (who played my boyfriend, Troy, who stalks me on the show). I said yes to the job and in the process, met people who have remained dear friends and colleagues.

Over and over again saying yes has led me to something exciting and new and surprising. If you're lucky, you will say yes to the point that you are forced to say no. And, yes, luck is a component of this business too.

I've been lucky and sometimes I have to say no. Sometimes I hate that I have to say no, something really amazing comes up that I'm dying to be a part of, and I have to make a decision based on money or loyalty - two things entirely worthy of prioritizing, by the way. I've also been lucky enough to be able to choose art over money.

My yes has evolved.

I was lucky enough to cross paths with Michael Patrick King a few years ago. He's the master storyteller behind *Sex and the City* and *The Comeback*. He had a brilliant idea for a show and wanted me to be the star. I said yes, of course, but it meant saying no to a project with one of my best friends and greatest collaborators, Becki Newton (Matt's sis), with whom I shared a brain on *Ugly Betty*. Michael Patrick King is not only a businessman and artist I look up to, but also someone whose philosophy rings true to me. He says, "follow the green lights." Recognize what is a "go" for you and embrace it. If they want you to play ingenues, do it. If they want you to play heroes, you're a hero. If you're the clown... well, you get it...

In order to say yes, evolved or otherwise, you need to be informed and confident. As Matt says in his appropriately titled "Hot Mess Vibes" chapter, "confidence goes a long way, in auditions, on set, in interviews with agents, in life, everything." You are no longer in Kansas anymore (or Texas), you are most likely in a city where the system has been set up and is constantly evolving. The business of acting is happening, and you need to say yes to learning it. Mastering it. As Matt says: "Be the hardest working actor in the room." You can send that self-tape in because you know (after reading this book) what is necessary to do it and do it well. You can say yes to being a clown in an audition because you are confident and well-trained in the art of acting. When it's go time, green lights, you are ready. Yes!

Now I'm doing what my idols back in high school were doing. I'm making plays, but on Broadway! I have two shows coming up and that means I'll be rehearsing all day, every day while still performing eight shows a week. It's an insane prospect, but also two incredible jobs, so what did I do? Yep, I said yes. When you're given an opportunity, when someone wants you, when the stars align: say yes.

I won't pretend like "yes" is all you need. Show business is also about luck, timing, talent, persistence, thick skin and hard work. I've known Matt Newton for years now. I trust him and what he has to say about the acting biz. I knew him as an actor, and hustler (we've all got to hustle for that yes sometimes) and now as one of the most popular acting teachers in NYC. Not everyone has the opportunity to say yes or no, but you can use this book to prepare you to get to that level. It may start with a script or a meeting. But without that yes, and the prep that backs that up, you will miss all the potential opportunities that await you.

I love Chapter 13 (Get Off Your Ass) because I believe in order to break in and stay in the business of show, it takes a world of yes. That means creating your own yes to being entirely you. Your project, your story, your showcase. After I finish my marathon theater undertaking, I'll take part in my most gratifying yes to date. Becki Newton and I will join our favorite TV writers Jon Kinnally and Tracy Poust for Michael Patrick King's CBS sitcom pilot *Fun*. We are cast as a brother and sister who run the family funeral home. This came to fruition because Becki and I decided we wanted to work together again and despite the intensely competitive market of network television, we brought the partnership to the powers that be in hopes it would spark something. We would "not let demons creep in and eat our souls." Becki and I said yes to each other, and so far, we've been met with nothing but yeses in return.

So, turn the page, and say yes!

- Michael Urie

Covid Update

Two months after publishing this book, the Covid-19 pandemic came to the U.S. and completely shut down the film and television industry, putting thousands of actors out of work, as we all figured out a way to move forward and make major life adjustments. Broadway, the heart of American theatre, is shut down, movies theatres have closed, film festivals are doing virtual screenings, agents and managers have closed their doors after being in the industry for many years. What is happening? Is this for real?

As of October 2020, SAG-AFTRA has released a set of safety protocols to allow productions to go back to work, including mandatory testing, everyone having to wear masks (except the actors when cameras are rolling), quarantining before and after shoots, smaller crews, and the cast and crew having to divide into "zones" to minimize exposure and maintain social distancing. It's going to feel different, but we have to adapt to the new normal. Actors who have been fortunate enough to work during this time are few and far between. Some shows have been successful, and some have had to shut down for days or weeks as actors have gotten infected. As we await a vaccine, TV shows are slowly resuming production, and actors are being cast via self-tape and virtual auditions (see chapter on Zoom auditions). The atmosphere has changed, and now you may be asked to audition for roles delivering the lines with and without a mask. Commercials are being shot in the actor's own living rooms, where actors are expected to be their own director of photography, production designer, grip, costume designer, and makeup artist. Welcome to Crazy Pandemic 2020.

It's a terrible time for the industry, but hope is on the horizon. As always, we adapt, and we will come back stronger. This virus rocked my entire acting studio, and then we pivoted and moved everything online, thus allowing actors from all over the world to enroll in our classes. I didn't expect to be teaching a student from the Ukraine (don't even know where that is), but my whole world changed and now somehow it's bigger. It's different. Now is the time to get out of your comfort zone, write your own script, create your virtual one woman show, and strengthen your acting muscles. Now is the time to take care of you. Make sure you are ready, make sure you are training, make sure you have the right equipment, and make sure you know what is happening in the industry, as it's changing everyday. But remember this: The world needs art, and we will be here when it returns. Oh, and please don't suck.

Introduction

Eight long years ago I wrote a book for actors called *10 Steps to Breaking into Acting,* which offers honest, practical advice to new actors pursuing a career in acting. Did you read it? No? Well, you suck then. I also wrote a lot of articles for *Backstage* on how not to suck. Read them. It will change your life. Well, not really.

This is a warning. If you don't want to work your ass off in your pursuit of being a professional actor, then read no further. Seriously. Get a reality show instead or start a YouTube channel, or become a TikTok star. Laziness has no place here. As I always tell my students, "Be the hardest working actor in the room." If you are sensitive don't read this book. This business isn't for sensitive people. You have to be tough, you can't be fragile.

This book is a bible on perspective, about what it takes to be a professional, paid actor at the highest level (and how to put in the training and hard work to compete for these jobs). If you want to pursue acting as a hobby, then so be it. But this is for people who want to make *money* from it, in a major market, and want to understand the ins and outs of the business, without the sugar coating. There's no homework here, no "workbooks," and no patting you on the head telling you how cute you are.

Now is the time to level up.

I have been an actor, a filmmaker, a writer for *Backstage*, an acting coach, an author, an on-set coach, a really good ping pong player, and have had career consultations with hundreds of actors through the years. I've lived in New York and Los Angeles and worked on a lot of sets. I have some things I want to say. And if you are sick of hearing it from me, I've also included some candid interviews with a talent agent, a TV and film casting director, an editor, and a youth talent manager.

Perspective is key.

There is some serious b.s. being slung out there, and actors are in desperate need of some guidance. I don't want you to be the actor who has spent $11,000 on casting workshops and has never been called in for a single audition. I was told once to buy colored paper clips to attach my cover letter to my headshot and resume, as that would be "wacky" enough to make me stand out. S'up ladies.

As of January 2020, there were over 532 scripted television shows, with at least 60 filming and casting out of New York, with original content being created by Facebook (not just for stalking your ex), Instagram, Apple, Snapchat, YouTube Premium (formerly YouTube Red), Disney+, and HBO Max. Streaming has taken over, with Netflix, Hulu, and Amazon putting out award-winning shows and films, making these newer platforms relevant and necessary. Actors have agents in different markets, are booking jobs from self-tapes from anywhere in the world (with lightning-fast turnaround), and actors are learning how to pave their own way by creating their own content. Old shows are being rebooted and revamped. There are shorter seasons, limited series and longer hiatuses, which unfortunately limits residuals and creates financial insecurity for actors trying to make a living. Actors used to rely on first-run residuals. Now they have to supplement their acting work by becoming a yogi or serving cinnamon buns to American Girl dolls. I did it for years (the buns, not the yoga). On top of that, recent tax laws prohibit actors who are employees to write off commission fees to their agents and managers, which means they will pay more in taxes at the end of the year.

The internet has changed casting. Casting directors used to go to stadiums to do those huge open calls. Now they frequently ask for submissions from tape... and you can be anywhere. Some casting directors don't even have offices and are doing all of their auditions via tape, especially if they are in a rush. Your self-taping skills need to kick ass. No excuses. Self-tape auditions (and now Zoom) allow actors to compete for jobs globally, not just locally.

Back in the day, pilot season would involve 30-40 pilots being cast in an 8-week window, with only 4-7 being picked up to series, and the others scrapped (basically becoming expensive home videos that nobody ever sees). Pilot season has changed, and instead of 2 busy months, actors are busy all year. There is no real "off-season." Streaming doesn't operate on a traditional casting schedule, and networks like Hulu, Netflix and Amazon are snatching up the pilots that are being passed on by big networks (ABC, FOX, NBC, CBS). Instead of sitting on a beach in Cabo knocking down Rum Swizzles, you are sitting by your phone waiting for your next episodic audition to come in. Or it's *not* coming in and you are writing (and overthinking) 30 drafts of an email to send to your agent to fire them or light a fire under their ass.

So here it is. A practical, no-nonsense, no b.s. approach to understanding the business of acting. Do me a favor. After you read this, pass it along to a friend in need. You're welcome. They're welcome, too.

Chapter 1: Video Killed the Radio Star
The TV, Film and Theatre Market

My first paying TV job was on a Comedy Central show called "Strangers with Candy." It was 1999, and nobody had cell phones yet (I miss it). At the time there were only a few shows on cable filming in New York, a few soaps and a "Law and Order" or two. I played a blind football player on the show, and all of my scenes were with Amy Sedaris. I had never been on set before, cable barely paid actors anything, and it wasn't considered a "good" gig. I think my agent made $90 commission on it for my two weeks of work. Nobody had heard of the show, my parents weren't sure whether to congratulate me or worry about me, but I was a "working" actor. The director had me practice the role by walking around Times Square with a blind stick. Not kidding. The show didn't do well until it went to DVD. Then it gathered a following. Then it went streaming, and the show became a huge success in its post-life, and now people still recognize me from it. I wouldn't be surprised if there was a reboot in the near future.

Streaming. Has. Changed. Everything.

This is a golden time for television. Everybody wants to be a part of it. There are amazing TV shows popping up on all platforms, which well-known actors are dying to be a part of. Apple is securing famous actors to headline their original TV shows (Apple TV+), as everyone is desperate for eyes on their platforms. Content is key. It makes perfect sense why Snapchat would want to take advantage of its millions of subscribers and try to put original shows in front of them (under the name "Snap Originals"). This gives creators and actors a new way of gaining employment.

And with all of this our union, SAG-AFTRA, is constantly adapting, making sure actors are protected as these new opportunities pop up. Right now, a "major performer" big guest star role on a SAG-AFTRA TV show pays at least $1005 for a one-day Guest Star, $5528 per week for a half-hour show (based on 5 days), and $8844 a week for an hour-long show (based on 8 days). For smaller co-star roles, the rates are obviously less for daily and weekly use. Unless you're famous and your agent is like, "Give him $10,000 a day." Much like commercials, it used to be that every time a TV show aired again, the actor would see a huge residual check. Now that everything is streaming, an actor can be on a TV show that is watched many times over and over and not profit from it. So, the union is making sure our rates compensate for that (and trying to keep up with the ever-changing market and non-advertising, subscription-based platforms). How long until we see TikTok stars headlining TV shows? Oh wait, the new "She's All That" reboot stars a TikTok star. Too late! Former successful actors are trying to sustain their careers from the revenue they get through giving personal shout outs through the Cameo app. Welcome to Crazy Town. All aboard!

Well known acting studios, which have offered traditional theatrical acting training for decades, are now forced to keep up by offering Zoom classes, as well as "How to Audition for TV" and "How to Self-Tape" classes, just to stay relevant in an ever-changing climate and prepare actors for professions in the current marketplace.

Film is changing. Film contracts for SAG-AFTRA productions are broken down into Theatrical (budget over $2,500,000), Low Budget (budget less than $2,500,000), Modified Low Budget (budget less than $700,000), Ultra Low Budget (budget less than $250,000), Short Project (budget less than $50,000), and Student Film (budget less than $35,000). This allows maximum flexibility for directors at all financial levels (and sometimes means deferred pay for actors, which I hate). Indie films with modest budgets aren't made as much anymore (unless Grandpa Ted, a first-time film director, finances it with his Social Security fund), because it's much more difficult to get distribution for independent films these days, especially a film with all new actors (no matter how good they are). It's all about balancing well-known actors with not as well-known actors, to ensure bankability and profit (and foreign sales). It seems like our movie theatres are overrun with big-budget comic book movies. With streaming, there is a bit more flexibility, as it's less about box office, and much more about "buzz." Look at *Stranger Things*. I remember coaching young actors who were auditioning for that show (then called *Montauk*), and I thought "this won't get picked up." Um…whoops. They did a nationwide search for that show, and the Duffer Brothers watched all the self-tapes from *everywhere* to find this very unique cast of actors.

It makes much more sense for a director to make a short film, and use that as a teaser for a big-budget film (or to get an agent to help them get a directing gig on an episode of a TV show), or as a calling card than it is for them to shell out $100,000 of their own money to make a feature film (that may never see the light of day). Those big distribution deals don't exist like they used to. It still happens, don't get me wrong, but it's just not as common. So, actors are feeling the brunt of it, and not getting the opportunity to audition for these meaty films as frequently. It's a television market now, and that's where the money is. Major film festivals are also feeling the brunt of it, as distributors are nervous about shelling out money for a distribution deal for a film that might not get seen. They have to worry about P&A costs (prints and advertising), which can really eat up the profit, all the while Netflix can swoop in and promote on its own platform for the entire world to see. Indie filmmakers would prefer to have their film seen by millions, as opposed to MAYBE playing a couple of weeks on a platform release in a few cities around the country.

Now theatre is where the good actors go to stay sharp, to be creatively fulfilled, and to work on meaningful material in between jobs. This involves Broadway, off-Broadway, off-off Broadway, cruise ships, Equity tours, non-Equity tours, regional theatre, staged readings, workshops, my mom's living room, and showcases. It doesn't pay much, if at all, but if it is well-reviewed, and a hot ticket, it can help the actors get in front of television casting directors. Broadway shows come and go, but actors can still make a good living being in the ensemble of a good, long-running Broadway show. Or even as an understudy. As an Equity performer in a Broadway show, actors earn a minimum salary of $2168 a week for an 8-show schedule (unless they are famous and earn a negotiated salary and possibly a percentage of ticket sales).

Young talented playwrights are adapting to the new landscape by learning how to adapt their skills for TV. A lot of undergraduate and graduate schools are now offering courses in "How to Make TV Money," as the need for good writers for prestigious TV becomes more and more important. Writers' rooms for TV shows are scouting these programs for good writers with a knack for pacing, sophisticated dialogue, plot turns, and good character development. Because good writing hopefully means awards. And awards mean viewers. And viewers mean money. Now playwrights can supplement their income by writing for a show, if they are lucky, while they are mounting a play.

If you live in New York and are represented by an agent or manager, you are auditioning for everything under the sun on Breakdown Services (a part of Actors Access) that your reps pass along to you. This includes Broadway shows, short films, episodics, bigger roles on shows in Los Angeles, regional theatre, as well as some feature films. If you live in New York and don't have an agent or manager, most likely you are auditioning for unpaid work, readings of plays, short films with deferred pay, music videos, student films (no pay, lucky if you get the footage), or maybe even a paid gig or two you find online through casting websites.

It's a hot mess, and you gotta weed out the good from the bad and get as much experience under your belt as you can to build up that resume.

Chapter 2: Bite and Smile
Commercials: Union vs. Non-Union

I've auditioned for over a thousand commercials in my time. I booked three. Sorry, four. One was a Canadian wild spot (whatever that is). One of those four was a national McDonald's commercial. I filmed it in 2006 in Central Park and was told to bring my own outfit (red flag). A huge crowd gathered as we set up the shot out on Sheep's Meadow on a beautiful fall day. I still remember the sweet scent of urine and desperation in the air. The cameras rolled, the director called, "Action!" and I sat there on the grass smiling, bopping my head, and chomping on a cold Big Mac with butter shellacked onto it (thanks to the food wrangler). Fifteen seconds later, the director yelled, "Cut," looked directly at me, and held up his middle finger. Awkward pause. I stifled a laugh, thinking he was kidding. He wasn't. Apparently, he didn't like what I was doing, and that's how he expressed it. So, we did it six more times, each one more and more humiliating, as even the crowd around the set was laughing. There were no lines, no direction, nothing. I kept thinking, "I went to Vassar College and studied Drama, I can't believe this is happening to me." I wanted to speak up, but I didn't. I bit my tongue. I left, convinced I was getting cut out of the commercial. I even called a girl I was dating on the way home to tell her about it, but before I could tell her, she told me she didn't want to see me anymore. Good times! I think she serves Chilitos at the Taco Bell near Times Square now.

Then, a few depressing weeks later (during which time I contemplated quitting acting), I got a text from a friend in California: "Are you in a McDonald's commercial?" And there it was. My commercial was airing, and I was in it. And you know what else? That commercial spun off into about six different commercials, wild spots (still not sure), industrial, network, holding fees, internet buyout, cable, and I ended up making around $50,000 (more money than I've ever made off of any acting job to this day). And I worked for exactly one hour and was lucky enough to have the director flip me off. I'm awesome!

Commercials aren't like that anymore. Actors can no longer count on a national commercial (or several) running for a long period of time (you are lucky if you get 13 weeks), making tens of thousands of dollars while they go off and do low paying theatre or audition for television and film, while avoiding taking side jobs as a bartender or waiter at American Girl (just me?). The trend now is internet marketing, social media, OTT ("over the top" media) streaming, non-union, and getting these little ads in front of everyone's eyes while they are surfing through their phones. SAG-AFTRA recently approved new agreements for commercials, creating new Upfront Use Packages to help the move to media platforms, which gives actors a buyout upfront in certain situations.

If you are non-union, you can still make good money. You can settle for a buyout for a few thousand dollars (not as much as with a major national union commercial, but still good), and they can basically do whatever they want with your image and use it for as long as they want (this could mean 5 years or forever). This means smaller budgets, no residuals, longer runs. Some actors are told by their agents to stay non-union simply so they can profit from this. In this situation, actors are basically negotiating for themselves (although some agents negotiate non-union spots), and have no protection about when (or if) they are getting paid, etc. It's the wild west. Be prepared to negotiate if they can use your image "in perpetuity," and potentially have a commercial conflict for the rest of your life. That means if you book a non-union Honda commercial that pays you a $2,000 buyout, and they can use your image forever, then you can never again audition for any other kind of car commercial for the rest of your life (that could potentially pay you a lot more). That's where the "commercial conflict" bites you in the ass. A lot of these jobs offer exclusivity for a predetermined amount of time (like one year), meaning you can't audition or appear in a competitor's ad for the term. Look at your contract closely.

For SAG-AFTRA (the on-camera actor's union that costs $3,000 to join plus semi-annual dues), and for big commercial casting directors, this is very frustrating, and undermines their power. Unions are there to protect actors (hours on set, usage limits, residual payments), negotiate contracts, and help actors make a living. Advertisers used to hire union actors

6

because they could trust that they were getting a higher caliber of actor. Not true anymore. Advertisers are paying less to casting directors, sometimes not working with agents and just posting a breakdown to Actors Access or Casting Networks, in an effort to cast quickly and avoid all of the rules, paperwork, and regulations that are put in place. And guess what? Actors will do it, so they will still get thousands of submissions! Some actors who used to be in the union are actually going Fi-Core simply to make money. Crazy, right? Fi-Core or "financial core" status is a distinction within the Screen Actors Guild allowing actors to work both union and non-union jobs. It basically means you can be in the union but you give up your union status (and it is really hard to get back in). To be honest, this is really looked down upon, as the union considers you a "scab actor," and you lose all the protection they fought so hard to get for you, as well as all of the benefits. It's not something I recommend.

A well-known commercial casting director (who didn't want to be named) describes it like this:

"There's a lot of non-union work. We are in such a weird time with the union with so much streaming media and social media and new media, and I think until it settles, the amount of work for actors and casting directors and producers is at an all-time low. I think it will right itself, it will just take a little time.

The new contract was ratified in April of 2019. The union came up with what they thought was a good bundling deal, and I don't know why it wasn't as enticing as they thought it would be.

We hit January 2019 and the business died in a way I've never seen in 15 years. Budgets are tight, nobody can guarantee that anyone will see anything, so they're shooting hands, feet, bodies, but no people. A lot of commercials don't have people."

As my student Stacey, a successful commercial actress, puts it: *"I booked more hand jobs than ever this year!"* Go get 'em, Stacey!

Chapter 3: Hit Your Mark, Say Your Lines and Don't Be Weird
What it's Really Like on Set

One of my first paid acting jobs was a guest-starring role on "J.A.G." I booked it after going to a pre-read, and then a callback (where I messed up my lines and had to stop the scene) with one director and one casting director in the room. I was nervous, totally focused on the acting, the words, the listening (whether or not my fly was open), and not messing up (too late). But I got it anyway. Yay! The next day, I showed up to set, and they told me I had to drive a forklift to a specific mark on the ground, jump off the forklift, salute, and then do the scene I did for the callback. They had a forklift consultant on set telling me how to drive it, a military consultant telling me how to salute properly, and on top of that, I had to hit my marks, remember my lines, and not completely suck, with the series regular staring at me the whole time. Nothing about this makes for good acting, as the acting was secondary to all the technical stuff. Four years of theatre school! Actors need immense concentration with all the chaos going on around them. For all the yogis out there: Namaste.

So, you booked the job! Awesome. You beat the system. Party time! Wait…oh shit. You have never been on a set before and have no idea what you are walking into. Wait…why are there 150 people standing around? Where do I stand? What time is rehearsal? Who is the director again?

Sets are a whole different ball game.

Here's what you need to know. You are stepping into a well-oiled machine, where everyone has a very important job at certain points throughout the day. It takes 150 people around 8 hours to do a two-minute scene on a huge budget TV show, and about ten days to shoot an episode of a one-hour drama. That one line you have been obsessing about for the past few days, and probably said over 1000 times and met with three different coaches to make sure you nailed it? Yeah, that line has now changed, as well as the location, character, and then they add 10 more lines and a monologue in a Southern accent. Oh fuck.

Before you panic, you need to understand something. It's all good. On a big-budget set, everyone knows exactly what they are doing.

Here's how it works.

<u>Rehearsal</u>

After you sit in your trailer for *a few hours*, you will be called to hair and makeup. After hair and makeup, you will sit in your trailer for *a few more hours*, then be brought to set for a private rehearsal. This is where you and the other actors (leads on the show) will stand around in a circle and read the sides. It will seem as if nobody has read them before (some haven't), and you will pretend you haven't been saying it in your head over and over a million times.

Once the director has heard it out loud, he will "block it" and show everyone where to stand and figure out how many shots it will take. Then he will do a "marking rehearsal" where he will call all crew members in to watch the scene. Again, you are still obsessing over your line, trying to act cool, and not completely and unabashedly over-rehearsed. I mean, it all leads up to this, right? Four years of drama school, hundreds of auditions, three agents dropping you, $11,000 in casting workshops, and now here you are, ready to say your line! No big deal.

After the crew watches (and rolls their eyes), you go back to your trailer and wait for *a few more hours* while they set up lights and the camera with the stand-ins (I once asked out Rory's stand-in when I worked on *Gilmore Girls*—hey, they're people too). At this point, they might break for lunch, and you might spill some pasta sauce over that Dolce and Gabbana shirt. Fuck. Then at some point, you actually film, for like *ten minutes* tops! Hurry up and wait.

<u>Some things you should know on set</u>

Who is an AD? Can you even talk to the director, directly? Can you talk to other actors on set? What about famous ones? Can you get a picture with them? What's video village?

The first person you should know is the AD, or *assistant director*. According to Wikipedia, "The role of an assistant director on a film includes tracking daily progress against the filming production schedule, arranging logistics, preparing daily call sheets, checking cast and crew, and maintaining order on the set."

So, basically, they are the person who keeps the train moving and starts fuming when you keep messing up your line.

The next person you should know is the *director*. They either met you at the callback or hired you from tape. They liked what you did, so don't change anything. When filming, they have so much to think about, and most likely you won't have much interaction with them anymore. Unless you completely screw it up. No feedback means you are killing it. It's okay to ask him or her questions but know your place on set. If you are a guest star, you only have a couple of takes (the regulars get to play around and have more takes). Read the room. If it's chill, then, by all means, ask some pointed questions. If everyone is stressed and they are losing light, keep your movement journal questions to yourself.

Video Village is the place where the producers, writers, director (and their random friends) gather to watch the external remote monitors, which show what the cameras are seeing on set. Sometimes it's in the same room, sometimes it's somewhere else. Meanwhile, they are talking to you through a walkie talkie. It's dark and quiet and they don't love having actors hang nearby. It's where all of the big decisions are made about sound, lighting, color, camera angles, hair and makeup, line changes, if you suck or not, whether the acting is strong and connected or if they need to do more takes, and anything else that's showing up on the screen.

The *script supervisor* is your best friend. He or she is dealing with all matters of continuity, as well as lines. He or she will tell you if you flub a line, or if you picked up a cup with your left hand or right hand in the last take. They will make you look like a superstar in the editing room. And even if not, a good editor will make it work (see my interview with Howard Leder at the end of the book). It's more than okay to call for a line while you are filming, and they are the people that will call it out for you. Everyone does it. Just take a breath and start the moment again. The breath is the moment that is needed for the editor to cut around it. Know the line and own it.

A caution about "selfies" on set

Don't take pictures on set, and don't ask to get your picture taken with the famous actors. It's just not cool. Everything is confidential, and actors don't want to be bothered in their downtime. I heard about an extra who took a selfie in the bathroom trailer on a Marvel show, geotagged the location, and two minutes later a PA came up to her and told her to take it down. Marvel actually called about it. Don't be that person. Save all pics for when the show airs. Confidentiality is key in the age of social media as everyone is worried about important plot points getting out there.

The shoot

When they bring you back to set, they will tell you the order of shots. They might start with your closeup, show you some pieces of colored tape on the ground (your "marks"), and then shoot it a bunch of times. The other actor will most likely be off-camera acting with you (and rolling his eyes at you), but if he is a big star, there is a good chance he will go back to his trailer and you will be acting across from a piece of tape attached to the side of the camera. Good times! Eat your heart out, Meryl Streep. I'm talking to a piece of tape!

Chances are you will get one or two takes (because it's not about you), with very little direction, then they will film the other actor's coverage in the scene, and that will be it! They will say, "That's a wrap on Weirdo #1," there will be a smattering of applause, the director will shake your hand briefly, and then you will ride the Q train home at 2am (local stops only) with a smile on your face. You are a working actor! Put it on the resume, collect your check (less 45% in agent and manager commissions and taxes), and let the offers start rolling in!

Here's all you need to know: Show up, know your lines, take direction, don't be crazy, take off the sauce (the overacting), and be ready for everything to change. Be the actor that can roll with the punches, be someone people want to work with. Please. Don't. Suck. You will be treated like royalty for a day—you will have your own trailer (where a table folds over the toilet), great catered meals, and you get to wear fancy clothes. Enjoy it. Don't complain. It may be a while before it happens again. Hopefully, you got enough screen time to put it on your reel (another chapter).

Intimate Scenes

There's nothing more awkward than doing intimate scenes on a set. If a show has nudity, chances are your agent has spoken with the producers and added a "nudity rider" to your contract, which lays out specifically which body parts can and can't be shot. Nowadays it's more important than ever for a production to have an "Intimacy Coordinator" on the crew, who will carefully choreograph the scenes with the actors so that everyone feels comfortable and safe. Their job is to make sure the entire sequence, whether it's a kissing scene or sex scene or nudity, is carefully worked through in a safe, mutually agreed-upon way. They are essential nowadays and becoming more and more frequent on film and television sets as of 2019. *The Deuce* on HBO was one of the first shows to hire an intimacy coordinator.

Once you wrap

Say thank you and get the fuck out of there. Don't stick around to watch the filming, don't go talk the director's ear off. Peace out and let them continue with their nutty day. The best thing you could do is be a consummate professional, nail your takes, be polite, and go on with your day. Then get a beer and celebrate. After all, getting an agent, getting an audition, getting pinned, booking it and then actually shooting it (and your role not getting cut), you have already beat the odds! A great reason to have that beer. You will run into that same director on a different project, and most likely he or she will remember you. Or even better, they will bring you back and you suddenly have a recurring role on your resume.

When it airs

Now you can post pictures on social media! #Blessed, right? Blast it out. "Hey, check me out as Jimmy the Creepy Thug on tonight's episode of *Blue Bloods*. Holla!" Total thirst trap. But just make sure you aren't cut out of the show first. What? Yep, happens all the time. Makes for a really awkward viewing party, an awkward conversation at Christmas with your relatives, and a lot of apologies on your social media posts. Oops! Still goes on the resume, though.

One-line roles are where a lot of actors get their start! These are the coveted co-star roles that show that you have earned the right to be on TV, and it goes front and center on your resume. No more high school theatre! You never know if it will become something bigger, unless your character gets shot in the face. Then, well, I don't think they are coming back.

Chapter 4: Auditioning for Dummies
The Casting Process

The most awkward audition I ever had was for legendary film casting director Avy Kaufman. In her office are posters from some of my favorite all-time movies. Well, today she was casting a Pepsi commercial, and I was auditioning for it. For the commercial, all the dudes had to sit on a chair and pretend to be riding a roller coaster...in their tighty whities (4 years of drama school). Holla! So, I went in, said hello to Avy, stripped-down, slated my name, sat in the chair, and began hooting and hollering as I moved from side to side, front and back. As the "roller coaster" was going down the hill, I threw myself back in the chair (fully-committed), shouted, "Woo!" (half-committed), and successfully whacked my head on the wall behind me (mostly committed). She stopped the tape, asked if I was okay, and then said, "please try not to hit the wall." Fun, right???

Auditioning blows.

The first project I wrote and directed was a short horror film called *Hide/Seek*. Did you see it? No? You can rent it on Amazon Prime. I wrote the film for two reasons. The first reason was I wanted to show my acting students how easy it is to create your own work (more on this later). The second reason was to shine a huge spotlight on the casting process, blog about it, and really get into the nitty-gritty of what matters and doesn't matter when submitting for projects. Actors can get really bogged down in trying to control how they are perceived, down to the color of their shirt (don't wear white, blue, black, red, orange, purple or pink by the way), and the amount of catch light in their eyes in their headshot. My mission was to demystify the entire process, and so I did (with the help of my casting director, Kimberly Graham, who I love).

I posted a breakdown online, both through Breakdown Services (the one agents and managers see), as well as on Actors Access and Backstage (the one any actor who can read and write a check can see). It was a four-day shoot, and I was casting four roles that would pay $100 a day. For a 12-hour day, that's about $8 an hour, which is about half of the current minimum wage. You know how many submissions I got? Four...thousand. Yup. One thousand per role. Talk about overwhelming. I can't even imagine what it's like on a huge project, or one of those "we are doing an open call" type things.

So, I scrolled through all the photos on Actors Access (on my phone, where the headshots are half an inch tall), and some were glaringly bad (still black and white), wrong age, terrible-picture-taken-with-a-bad-camera type of ones. Many looked like dating site reject photos, and some were shirtless (I mean....). When the pictures are that small, by no means am I blown away by the $1500 headshot. I couldn't even tell you which one that was. Everyone started to look the same. Then there were the headshots that were good, the right type, but they had no video attached to their profile. Pass. Why would I want to spend five days with you on my passion project without seeing any video of you first? Put up a slate shot and two scenes of footage (like right now)! What actors need to understand is that if you have a slate shot and footage and a comment ("I'm a real nurse," "I'm a stuntman," "I'm actually homeless"), your headshot goes to the top of the 4,000 submissions and weighs more heavily (truth bomb).

I wanted to bring in about 20 actors, but I wanted to be sure they were *right.* So I *only* looked at actors who I either knew (from a previous class of mine) or who I could gauge their talent through their video footage. If I liked their look, then I clicked on the *slate shot,* which tells me what they *really* look like, and how they sound (and is no more than 7 seconds long). Do they look like their headshot? How do they sound? If I was still interested, I would click on *media.* It didn't matter what the footage was from, just that I *got a sense* of their talent. It didn't matter if it was from a huge film, or an "audition style" self-tape scene in front of a gray wall (you hear that, actors?). And then I went through the submissions from agents and managers, who had actors with lots of credits, Tony nominations, the whole deal.

Here's where the casting process gets interesting. Instead of blindly bringing 20 actors into the room who you aren't sure are right for the job, casting directors can now go through all of the submissions, whittle down the ones who are physically right for the part, and then request a self-tape from those actors to see how they approach the material. All *before* they have even stepped into the casting room. It's like a pre-pre-read. At this point, the casting and creative team can scroll through tapes whenever and wherever they want, watch a few seconds of one (that's all you really need), skip others, and make their choices based on *already liking their work.* So, by the time the actors are in the room, they already have been vetted. They are rooting for you. Once you realize the casting director is on your side, everything changes. You feel supported and confident. Especially if they bring you back every time there is a role that is right for you. This system happens more with films, or even pilots, where there's a longer audition process. Episodic television happens so fast that there isn't time to look at a bunch of tapes (unless you are auditioning from out of town and then they might book you from tape).

What's an "in the room" audition like? Well, put it this way: *super* awkward. Every room is either ice cold or wonderful and welcoming, sometimes there is a chair, sometimes there is not (so practice the scene both sitting and standing), sometimes the reader is standing on the opposite side of camera than what you imagined (so practice both ways), sometimes they are drawing a mustache on your headshot (happened to me), sometimes the reader sucks, sometimes you have to wear a lavalier microphone, and sometimes they forget to turn the camera on after you did the best acting of your life. Party time. Every actor needs to learn how to walk into a room with confidence and audition with nothing but their imagination. There are very few people who make it look easy. Take a class, practice with different scripts, learn about eyelines, audition etiquette, how to slate like you aren't crazy, and how to not sabotage your audition by talking too much. You feel me?

With self-taping becoming the new normal, actors can submit auditions anytime and anywhere from all over the world. Knowing how to make a quality self-tape quickly is mandatory for every actor. You know what else is interesting? On my last short film, I requested self-tapes from about 200 actors who I really liked. Guess how many actually sent them in? 103

and a half (one forgot to send in one of the audition scenes). Get it together, people! Some people forgot or missed the deadline, or simply changed their mind (or hated my script. Hi, mom!).

After the pre-read is the *callback*, where you sit in a hallway clusterfuck of actors with flop sweat, waiting for your chance to go in and bomb in front of the producers, after which you will go over the scene a million times in the elevator wishing you had done it differently, call your parents and tell them you are quitting, take up a new hobby, break up with your girlfriend, all before you make it out to the car/subway/Uber. Just me?

At this point, there are a few people in the room you should know. There is the *writer* (who is also a producer), the *director*, the *casting director*, the *casting assistant*, and always some random dude with a laptop in the corner (they don't have an actual name).

For episodic television, the creative team is seeing a few people for each role, they are probably casting about 10-20 roles for the whole episode, which works out to about 50-100 people at the callback casting session. They are also probably racing back from a location scout, and then have to do a concept call after the casting. Why am I telling you this? Because I need you to understand something.

It's. Not. About. You.

The casting process sucks, and actors overthink it. They have seen so many people in a day, and each actor is coming in for their big moment, to prove how great they are, and to show mom and dad and Grandpa Ted that they are making the right decision. One minute after you leave the casting room you are already forgotten. Even if you were the best actor they've ever seen. I mean it. Don't worry if they didn't give you a redirect, if they didn't smile, shake your hand, punched you in the face, gave you new sides five minutes before, or told you that you remind them of Al Pacino (the older, more crazy version). You could still book the job!

So, what's an actor to do?

Do your work, show up, walk into the room with confidence (more on this later), relax, present your version of the scene, act like you are in your living room, take direction if they ask, leave the room gracefully (don't ask to do it again or stay and talk about *The Marvelous Mrs. Maisel*), throw out your script, and then crawl under a rock and ball your eyes out. No wait, that's not right. Go get a damn ice cream (or a martini) and treat yourself, because you just did your job. Take the pressure off, go have fun, stop overthinking. You will be auditioning for the rest of your life, so learn to enjoy it, and stop worrying about getting a gold star. You are a professional who has a certain skill set. If those are the skills they need and you fit their idea of the character, then great. If not, then move on and show your skills to someone else. But stop acting like you don't deserve to be there. It's not cute.

And also? Here are some reasons you didn't book the job: "too handsome, too sexy, a bit short, too relatable, a bit gay, not gay enough, not cross-eyed enough, a bit doughy, reminds me of my mom, too hairy, not hairy enough, jaw too square, I like potatoes, nose too perfect, and were his shoulders sloped?" In other words, so much of casting has nothing to do with talent and is completely out of your control. So, since you can't control it, why not just go in and have a good time? Maybe the casting gods will smile on you, or maybe it's the other guy's turn. Oh well. Onward and upward, right? Sometimes your "vibe" is right for the part, which is something that is completely unexplainable. And guess what else? If you are in the room, that means you are good. Everyone is good! It just comes down to chemistry and who matches well with the other actors in the project. When I was casting my last film *Sins of the Son*, I requested one hundred self-tapes, brought in the twenty who I felt nailed the material, and at the end of that audition, it was almost impossible to choose. Every girl who came in was amazing. So, we had to choose, and we went with "vibe." And I emailed every actress who came in to let them know how good they were, because I didn't want them to think they did something wrong. But I wouldn't expect that ever, because it never happens. After the actors are cast, it's "go" time, and there is rarely time to look back, reconnect, or think about actors who weren't cast. But maybe, just maybe they will think about you for something else, because you remind them of their mom or because you had just the right amount of hair.

The point is, the casting process is whack, you are standing in front of a neutral wall using your imagination to trick the casting director, or producer, into believing that what you are experiencing is real, and the whole thing is all very strange. Sometimes you have to pretend you are dancing at a club with an imaginary Pop Tart, and sometimes you have to ball your eyes out at the top of the scene, and other times you have to pretend you are watching your friend get shot in the face. Fun! So how do you do it? How do you cultivate that moment at home, and then make it real when it matters? I'm sure you can trick yourself into tears when you are at home by yourself, or even in a self-tape (by using a "cry stick"), but can you do it tomorrow at 4pm in front of the casting director, then next Tuesday at 12:30pm for the producers, then 10 times the next day on set? You have to train consistently so that you are ready for anything and can really dive into your imagination over and over again.

Some people are great at auditioning, and some suck. It's a separate muscle than talent. That is why self-taping is wonderful because it allows the actor to control the outcome. But when self-taping isn't an option, the stakes are higher, and nerves can get in the way. Dun dun dun!

Chapter 5: When in Doubt, Zoom in
Auditioning in Your Underwear

We were in class and two people were up doing a chemistry read style scene over Zoom. All of the other actors in the class had their cameras and mics off - or so we thought. Halfway through the scene we heard the voice of a class member who started talking, something along the lines of: "No. It's just not working anymore. It's not you, it's me. I just think it's time to move on." An actor in class had forgotten to turn off her mic and she was breaking up with her boyfriend mid scene. Fun times!

I had never even heard of Zoom before this year, and now it's all that anyone ever talks about (I really wish I had invested in some Zoom stock). Right now, casting directors aren't seeing actors in person at all. It's too risky. They are either casting directly from tape or are doing live auditions and virtual callbacks via Zoom, WeAudition, or BlueJeans. The creative team is now on the other side of the screen staring at you through the computer. Fun! And hey, you can wear your Batman underwear, and they won't even notice! Unless, of course, they are like "Can you try the scene again, standing this time?" Oops. Yup, it happens.

So hide the weird doll collection in your mom's basement behind your flex backdrop and buckle up because it's going be this way for a while and I want you to master the art of online auditioning. Do you know where your eye line should be when reading with someone over Zoom? Do you know how to adjust your sound and exposure manually through the Zoom setting so you can be seen and heard clearly? Do you have a good HD webcam? How do you do a standing scene without balancing your laptop on some old acting books or some oversized bundle of toilet paper you thought you needed but didn't? Your lighting, framing, internet speed, backdrop, Zoom etiquette, and on-camera acting matter more than ever. Standing out on a computer screen is different than popping in a self-tape. Here's everything you need to know about mastering your next Zoom audition. Print it, write it down, laminate it and use it as a mousepad.

Use your laptop or desktop

Always, always do online auditions on a laptop or desktop and not on a smartphone. Make sure you have the latest software update, as it allows for maximum flexibility for you. You can adjust your exposure, cut out the sound of your roommate snoring in the background, and also "touch up your appearance" so you don't look like a hot mess (my favorite). You can even do a split screen and have your sides on the computer at the same time (but honestly you should be memorized, right?).

Invest in a tripod laptop stand

This will allow you to raise and lower your computer so that you can do both standing and sitting scenes. They go for around $50 on Amazon. If you use a music stand, your laptop will slide off of it. I know an actor this happened to. Totally broke their computer. Good times!

Pay attention to sound

Wear some kind of earbud with a microphone, or use an external USB mic when reading as it avoids your dialogue cutting out in Zoom when overlapping with your lines in a scene. Without earbuds, you'll miss cues, not hear lines, and it'll make for a very frustrating read. Also, by having the earbud mic close to your mouth, it mimics using a lavalier microphone and picks up the subtlety in your voice.

Upgrade your internet

Now more than ever your internet needs to be strong and consistent. Create your Zoom set up in the area with the best wireless to avoid it being glitchy.

Make sure your laptop camera is 1080p

If you have an older computer, your camera won't be as crisp at 720p. To fix this, use your smartphone as a web camera by downloading the EpocCam app ($7.99), or buy an affordable 1080p or 4k webcam. Put your camera on a small tripod behind your computer. It's a total game-changer that gives crisp, clear video, works seamlessly with Zoom, and will really make you pop.

Know your eye line

You want to recreate the feeling of being in an in-person audition, not that you are doing a vlog for your new YouTube channel. The best way to do this is to look just left or right of the camera. You can either put a piece of tape on the corner of your laptop, or even better, minimize your Zoom window and put your reader on the top corner of your screen. I think it's always better to look someone in the eye for an audition rather than blankly staring at a piece of tape. Although, sometimes that piece of tape is a better reader than most casting directors. Oh, snap!

Invest in decent lighting and a solid backdrop

No virtual backdrops of you knocking back a Vodka Tonic on a beach. These can be the same ones you use as your self-tape setup. Invest in two soft boxes, a gray or blue backdrop, a hair light, and a backdrop light of some kind (Google "four-point lighting") if you want to really seem professional. In a perfect world, you're using your Zoom setup and your self-tape setup as one area and just swapping out the tripod with your laptop with your phone or camera tripod set up (these are two different kinds of tripods).

Own it

The casting director is now coming into your world, your safe space, and you're inviting them to see your art. You're on your home turf. I always used to say to actors before they went into the room for their auditions, "act like you are in your living room." Now you are there. Literally. I notice nerves dissolve as actors use the environment effectively around them. Most of us are at a desk, which allows us to lean forward, put our elbows up, creating more intimacy with the camera, drop our voice way down, and focus on maximum subtlety. I've seen actors tape their sides to their ring light (whatever works, right?). They can lean back in their comfortable chair and put their feet up, allowing them to create more of a physicality around their characters. I've noticed actors using things on their desks (a pen, a notebook, a bottle of water) as essential parts of their scenes, and it totally works. They're able to create their environment in a much more vivid way, bringing in their essence and really killing it.

Casting director Jenny Ravitz ("Chicago Med", "Chicago PD") sums it up like this: *"Take the time to settle any nervous energy before your Zoom audition. Things might go wrong - the wifi can cut out, you can't hear the director, your reader gets confused which scene to start on. It's okay to ask for what you need. You can always politely ask the director to repeat his adjustment or show your reader the correct page. We know that this isn't the norm!"*

Do's and Don'ts of Zoom Auditions:
- Do wear pants. Please.
- Ring lights are okay, as long as you supplement with soft boxes or LED lights.
- Make sure your laptop camera is eye level.
- Don't wear bulky headphones, as it's distracting.
- Light a candle and pray your internet doesn't cut out mid-monologue.
- Hide your kids in the basement.
- Make sure you know where the "mute" button is in case your boyfriend breaks up with you mid-audition.
- Be prepared to sit in a virtual waiting room for a while.
- Don't get too comfortable. Nervous energy is good.
- Remember that casting directors are in your corner and they are figuring this out too.

- Allow for mistakes and soldier through without saying "I'm sorry."
- Test your video and audio before the meeting. Don't be that guy.

Online auditioning will be here for a while. You will be doing chemistry reads over the computer with other actors. Strange times, indeed. Practice in a class where you get used to the Zoom interface and get comfortable with the new online audition etiquette so you are ready when that next audition comes up! You got this!

Chapter 6: Hot Mess Vibes
On Dealing with Nerves and Confidence

I have a "Sorry Jar" in my acting studio (MN Acting Studio). Every time an actor says "Sorry" in the middle of a TV or film scene in class, they have to put a dollar in it (it's my wine fund). If they don't have a dollar, they have to Venmo it to the studio. Why? Because actors need to stop apologizing. It's gross, unnecessary, and a waste of everyone's time. It's the acting equivalent of chewing your nails.

Nerves make actors tense. Tension gets in the way of actors being themselves. We've all been there--hands shaking, palms sweating, rushing through lines, and disconnecting from the world of the scene. Nerves come from actors wanting to get a job so bad that they actually are thinking about that instead of doing the scene. Instead of being present, they are micromanaging the future while they are in the room (how much money will I make from this? will my agent drop me?). The more present you are, the calmer you will be. The more you do the work, visualize the scene, and focus on the specifics, and really see it, the more grounded you will be. All you have to do is focus for 30 seconds or a few minutes when you are in the audition, then you can resume your nutty thinking. But learn how to lock it down.

This is why people take classes, both in acting and in auditioning. They are working the acting muscle every week so that when they audition or arrive on set, they are a well-oiled machine, ready to do the work. I even think improv is an incredible skill that teaches actors to roll with the punches and be spontaneous and get out of their head. Improv helps actors build confidence, learn how to think and feel in the moment, push themselves outside of their comfort zone, and develop muscle memory so they can step into any situation and face it dead on.

Confidence goes a long way, in auditions, on set, in interviews with agents, in life, everything. So many actors walk into rooms with their shoulders hunched, as if they are already apologizing for something they haven't done yet, like they *expect* their audition to suck. It's not cute, and it makes people not want to hire you. You need them to *trust* you, and they need to feel that they can put you on set opposite a major star, say two lines, and not have a panic attack and fall apart. I know a casting director who says if an actor's hands are shaking in the audition, there's no way she can put that actor opposite the lead of the show. Here's an audition hack: put something heavy underneath your sides, like a notebook. It prevents your hands from shaking and makes you seem really confident. You're welcome.

What is the right amount of confidence and how do you get it? You get it by working on developing the *skills* required to be an actor. Some people learn by going to a conservatory, some learn by taking weekly classes, and some learn by simply acting on set. This means you can trust that you can walk into any sterile casting office, or onto any set, and simply *act*, without any fear, inhibitions, uncertainty, or any desperation. It's a very hard, tricky thing to master, but it makes all the difference in the world.

The best, most successful actors are the ones who work on themselves and are so grounded, so relaxed, and treat every audition as just another chance to show what they do, without any need to get anything from it. They are calm, poised, confident in their ability, effortless, and they completely let it go when they leave the room. We all need to emulate this.

I've seen many actors lose out on jobs because their nerves got in the way. They brought anxiety into the room because they either haven't had an audition in a year and "this is a big one," or they are worried about paying their rent. All of those thoughts make actors tense, less creative, they are unable to take direction as quickly, and ultimately it makes them try too hard in their auditions. If I am describing you, then you need to find a way to let that go (or disguise it), so that casting directors and producers can feel at ease when you are in the room. They need to trust you. That's what it's all about. Because if you are a hot mess in an audition with just two people in the room, how are you going to be on a set with 150 people?

If you grasp this concept, your perspective will change. You will not *need* every job you audition for, you will stop *desperately* trying to please the casting director, and you will *relax* into the idea of "I am just here to show you my work, and my interpretation." You have a unique fingerprint that you can put on the scene, and nobody can mess with that, or change what is inherently unique about you (it's your DNA). If you understand that, your auditions will be easier, and you will be more relaxed in the room. Because you aren't competing with other people, you are simply there to say, "I wonder if this is what you are looking for? Because this is my take on the role."

That alone will make you a more interesting actor. Confidence, not arrogance.

Even the most successful working actors develop anxiety later in their careers, as they feel a stronger desire to "live up" to the work they have achieved.

Once again, it's all about perspective. What matters to you? Why are you putting so much pressure on this? Learn to shift your focus so that the work speaks for itself, and you don't take it personally. Act like every audition is your first one, release the need to book the job, and just have a good time for a few minutes. Easy, right?

Chapter 7: Cue Cards and Cry Sticks
The ABC's of Self-Taping

I once watched an actor's blurry self-tape with a cat chilling on the bookshelf in the background. That cat was awesome, so engaged, listened really well, and was camera ready. Wish I could say the same for the actor, who was half in the dark, half memorized and looked like he was halfway through a 36-hour bender. Seriously, did this guy not hear of W.C. Fields' famous quote, "Never work with children or animals" because they will always steal the show.

No more sucky self-tapes. Please.

Self-tapes are the new pre-read. Get good, people. It's better for everyone. It's all about production value, performance, and your essence. You can take as long as you want, watch it back many times, see everything that works or doesn't work in your performance, do a screening for your grandmother, and most importantly, you can literally act in your living room without nerves getting in the way. It's awesome and allows actors to be at their personal best, which is the best way to gauge talent. Actors are testing for pilots from tape and booking television gigs from tape. Globally, not just locally. The competition is fierce. Own it, kill it, stop making excuses.

How many self-tapes do you do a week? How many of them suck? The next time you get a self-tape request, I want you to remember something. When you are tired, hungover, and your 50 year old roommate is asking you to set him up with a meeting with your agent, you have to memorize ten pages, and look like you just stepped out of a burned up forest, remember this: someone else, who is up for the same role, is going into a professional studio. They are camera-ready (sometimes bringing their own makeup artist), fully memorized with professional lighting and sound, reading with another actor, who is also bringing out a great performance. They are ready to step into the role at that moment. You can just tell. So, stop sending in bad self-tapes! Your agents and managers will not send it to casting and they will question your audition skills, your talent, and not want to pitch you, because they can't trust you. You feel me?

There is no excuse for sending in a poor-quality tape. As actors, so many things are out of our control and this is *one* thing that is not! You can literally do it on your phone (use a tripod and iPhone adaptor, and film horizontal please). Everyone from anywhere now has the ability to throw their hat in the ring, call themselves a "local hire," and send in a beautiful tape with the most basic equipment. Jimmy is in a hotel room in Punta Cana sending in a self-tape for 2 lines on *NCIS*, because Jimmy remembered his lavalier and portable tripod with attachable light. Get with it! Again, people, jobs are cast from tape. Actors are testing for pilots from tape. It's the new norm.

Here's what you will need: two softbox lights with daylight bulbs, a gray sheet for a backdrop, a cheap lavalier microphone to hook up to your phone, iMovie editing software, a Dropbox, WeTransfer or Hightail account, and someone who doesn't suck to read with you. You can have the nicest looking tape on the planet, but if the person reading with you isn't giving you much to play off of, is too loud, or has a weird distracting accent, it will affect your read (you hear that, mom and dad?). *You* can control the outcome, which gives you the power here. You aren't going into an audition room and praying you nail it on the first take. You can spend 10 hours on this if you want. Later in the book, when I sit down with casting director Stephanie Holbrook, take note of her comments on self-tapes.

Take all the time in the world! Pay attention, I'm going to break down the most important parts.

Lighting

Lighting is key. Invest in two softbox lights from Amazon (I like the Limostudio lighting kit), and place them on either side of the camera, slightly higher than eye level. This will create a nice "catch light" effect in each of your eyes, making them twinkle. This also helps with shadows and replicates natural light from a window. If you are feeling really crazy, put a small light behind you to light up the backdrop, as this will separate you from the back wall, remove shadows behind you, and make you "jump" off the screen. Ring lights are very popular, but be careful, as they can make you look "catlike." Play around with formations, create dimension with the lighting. Avoid making yourself look "flat and washed out." Nice shadows are flattering. Overhead shadows make you look like that dude from *Saw*. Film yourself, watch it back (on a computer if you can, not just on your phone). Lighting and color are different on televisions and computers and phones, and you want to check it everywhere. Make it perfect and foolproof so you are ready any time these last-minute tapes come in.

Backdrop

Gray is the current trend. Green screens make it look like you are in a weird exhibit at a kid's museum. So, paint a wall or hang a flat curtain without wrinkles. Don't film in front of a white wall because it messes up the white balance of the video. Google it. The less messy the better. You don't want anything distracting the viewer from your face. So maybe don't film it in your bedroom with your *Acting for Dummies* book in the background and your cat sleeping on the shelf? Neutral and flat, so that absolutely nothing distracts from the actor.

Sound

Sound is so important. A good performance is unwatchable if the sound sucks. Whether you are using your phone or a DSLR camera, invest in a small lavalier microphone (about $20 on Amazon-I like VidPro), so that the sound of the actor is crystal clear, and thus the reader is softer. The worst thing you can do is have a loud reader. No matter how good they are, a loud reader screws up a tape and distracts the viewer. Experiment with this, play around with how far away the reader stands so that they aren't drowned out or sound like they are in another room. All anyone wants is for this to sound like a normal conversation, with an emphasis on the person who is actually being seen. I've seen some odd self-tapes from kids too. There was a memorable one where their mom was literally screaming off-camera and acting up a storm. Take off the sauce, mom.

Camera

Use your iPhone or use a good DSLR with autofocus. Everyone has a smartphone, and everyone can take high-quality video now (especially with an app called Filmic Pro), so there is no excuse for a poor-quality, blurry self-tape. It's amateur. A small investment can go a long way in your professionalism and ability to book jobs. THIS is in your control!

Framing

The camera should be eye level, or even slightly higher. The camera should never be looking "up" at the actor. The frame should be a medium shot (chest up), with a little room above the head. Know your frame when you are filming so you don't pop in and out of it. If you are filming with your cell phone, the video MUST be horizontal (use a tripod iPhone adapter). The frame should include only you, not the edges of your backdrop. For full-body shots in a slate, you can shoot waist up and pan down. If you are adding a slate, I highly recommend filming it separately, and then put the files together in iMovie. It gives the actor a chance to reset before the actual audition scene, especially if the scene begins with some serious emotional stuff.

What happens when you are in a Motel 6 hotel room and your cheap tripod doesn't work? This is where you get creative. Put your phone on some books, face it towards you, swap out some bulbs, and you can make it look EXACTLY the same. Play around. I've seen some actors be very crafty with this.

I know someone who had to film a self-tape with a full-body shot and had nobody to help her (sad face). She attached a piece of string to the handle of the tripod and was able to pan the camera down to do the full-body shot while recording.

Eyelines

Always put the reader slightly right or left of the camera. Do you have a good side? Pay attention to it, Mariah Carey. Always film on that side. It matters. Never look right into camera, unless it's a slate and they ask you to. If a new character enters frame, put them on the other side of the camera from the reader. Create the world, see everything around you and react accordingly. Nobody needs to know you are in your mom's basement. Let me paint a picture for you: You are standing in line at a restaurant, waiting to place your order with the person behind the counter. The man in front of you engages you, but then you are taking to the person behind the counter and then you are reading a menu on the wall...where are your eyelines? Who's the reader? Where's the menu? Picture the scene. The casting director wants to feel like they dropped you into the restaurant and the scene unfolds. They can see it. You can feel it.

Upload and Edit

Once you get the good takes, edit it together in iMovie, compress the file, and upload it to a sharing service. And oh man your wifi better be working. I know someone who filmed a perfect self-tape and went to upload it right before the deadline, realized their wifi was out, missed the deadline and wasn't able to submit it. And don't ask your agents for extensions. They don't like it. It means they have to ask casting, and casting has to tell the producers. It's a whole thing. Just get it done on time.

Every actor needs to know how to do this with very little notice. You should know basic editing, how to put the takes together in the timeline, adjust the sound for any excessive "room noise" or "hissing," compress the file so it's under 500 MB, and then share the file to Vimeo, Dropbox, WeTransfer or Hightail. Period. You could get an email tonight at 9pm from your agent asking for a self-tape due the next morning that has 15 pages of sides. Get used to it. No excuses. This is the big leagues, yo.

So, no more overhead lighting, shot in your bedroom handheld-selfie-style, with your creepy American Doll collection in the shot. It makes people question your sanity and not want to work with you.

Essence

Let's get to the most important part of a self-tape (and auditioning in general). Because you don't have the luxury of being in the casting room, saying hello, making dumb jokes about traffic, and showing some personality before your audition (which a lot of actors prefer), you now have to let your personality shine through in the tape. By personality, I mean your *essence*. When you first read for a project on tape, you must, must, must allow your *essence* to come through. You want to show them who you are, quirks and all, and your take on the character. Don't worry about every little inflection, don't worry about what's "right," just make some strong choices, have a point of view, and show your work. It should be relaxed, not overly memorized or coached. If you have the right *essence* for the character (something you can't control), there's a good chance they will ask for a re-tape with very specific notes (a callback). In this case, they will give you a list of things to do differently, such as what color to wear, how to say certain lines, the whole deal. This is where you want to nail it.

So, let's be clear. When you get a request for a self-tape, no more worrying about perfection. It only inhibits you and makes you look like a robot. Robots aren't interesting. Robots don't pop off the page. Sit in on a casting if you ever get a chance, and watch 50 people try to do it "right," and then watch the actors who are so comfortable with themselves and their talent, that they are speaking these lines as if they are *theirs*, saying them as if it's the first time, with no pushing, no forcing, no "acting," and see which one you prefer. Remember, it's not about the lines, it's about the moments in *between* the lines, the non-verbal ones, where you can speak volumes about your character without saying anything. Sometimes that's as simple as a little smirk, a small sigh, or a nervous laugh. In a sea of people saying the same damn lines, those are the things that stand out.

And those little things only come out when the actor is relaxed, listening, and letting his or her *essence* come through.

A true "self" tape

Learn to do a self-tape by yourself. Yes, with no reader. Trust me. There will be times where your roommate is out at the clubs and won't be able to read with you on your tape. In these instances (worst case scenario), I want you to do this: use the Voice Memo app on your phone (or Line Learner, or Rehearsal Pro), and record the other person's lines, leaving room for your own. Put that phone right next to your camera, as if it's the reader. No, I'm not kidding. Yes, you will need a second video recording device, like your computer. I've assigned this as an exercise for my class, and sometimes you can't even tell the difference between having a reader there and the voice memo. Figure it out and get good at it. You will thank me later. I know students who have booked jobs from this. To make this work, you have to make sure there is a clear difference between the character you are playing and the "character" of the reader. If it sounds like the same person, it will be jarring. Play with it. Differentiate. But hey now, don't get too crazy.

I love self-taping actors in my studio because we have full control and we can use all the tricks in the book to get the performance. One of the best parts of self-taping is that nobody sees what goes into it. I know actors who put up cue cards on either side of camera, and others who use the famous "cry stick" (a lipstick-sized menthol stick that makes your eyes well up when you put it below your eye), and others who do 30 jumping jacks before rolling camera because the character is "out of breath." Side note: read the directions on the cry stick so that you don't go blind. Basically, you get to do the things you aren't supposed to do in an in-person audition. Whatever works, right?

Work harder than anyone else. Don't be the person who sends in a tape right at the deadline. Send it in a day before. People are looking at tapes in real-time, as they come in. Don't wait until the last minute. It may never get seen! Yup, you did all that prep, you did all that work, memorization, lighting perfection, sold your soul for a good reader and sent it in at the deadline and it was never seen. Because there were actors who sent it in the day before you, and at tape number 200, they stopped. Be better, be quicker, be the hardest working actor in the room, get your prep time down so you can knock out a kickass self-tape within a few hours.

Chapter 8: The Art of the Deal
Agents and Managers

When I started, I sent out my dumb ass black and white headshot to hundreds of agents. A few called me in and started "freelancing with me" (which basically means they offered to submit me on the official breakdowns in the hopes of getting a tug). Sometimes they got me auditions, but it was rare (maybe a once monthly MTV promo audition for little money, sometimes a film). I was temping every day (not fun--lots of filing papers for no reason and dreaming of stardom). After four months of freelancing, one of these agents got me in for an audition at a big casting office. I almost booked this big film and the casting director recommended I meet with a big manager. That big manager signed me and brought me to a big agency, which gave me a contract. That agent sent me to LA for pilot season for three weeks and I screen-tested for my first pilot within a month of being out there, then ended up staying for 8 years and working consistently in TV and film. Bye-bye temp work! If I didn't get into that big casting office, I would have had a different path. But the goal was always the same: make them notice you.

At this moment you either have an agent or manager you are happy with, are thinking of finding a new one, are sort of freelancing with one but they never call you back (agent freelancing happens more in New York but not in LA), or you are looking for one for the first time (or the millionth time because you just haven't found "the one"). Everyone needs an agent or manager if they realistically want to have a professional acting career and make money. These are the industry unicorns that have access to the breakdowns, who represent a select group of actors, and submit them on a daily basis for potential job opportunities. They are the people who will call casting on your behalf and pitch you if they believe in you.

A talent *agent* works for a talent *agency*, which can represent anywhere from 50 to 500 actors. An agency can have one agent or dozens. They take a 10% commission on everything only *after* you have booked a job (never pay upfront). So basically they work their asses off for free most of the time for many people, desperately trying to open up doors for them, only to sometimes walk away with a $90 commission for two weeks of work. And actors are *always* pissed at their agents. Save the drama for your mama.

Agents spend most of their time submitting, calling, emailing, making deals, negotiating contracts, and in the case of the bigger ones, have very little time to go over your thousands of headshots, your hours of demo reel footage, or to talk to you about what you are having for dinner. Contracts can be a year to a year and a half in length to start, after which they can be renegotiated for longer terms. In some cities, like New York, an agent can enter into a freelance contract with you, which means you are testing the waters before signing an official contract. It's like dating. You can date a few different agents if you want. Sometimes an actor will freelance with an agent, and not hear from them, and sometimes an actor will get a bunch of auditions. If the agent is happy, they might request to sign you exclusively. So, basically actors can freelance with a bunch of agents in the hope that one of them gets them an audition. LA is a bit different. More jobs, more agencies, more opportunities, and agents sign actors exclusively (meaning they can't "date" other agents). There will be more one-off jobs on TV shows out in LA because there are more TV shows than film out there (casting directors in Los Angeles will only see New York actors via self-tape if it's a bigger guest star, recurring, or series regular role).

A talent *manager*, however, is more hands-on, more in the know, more aware of your feelings, and able to offer an additional push (for an additional 10-20%) to get you into rooms. Most managers are part of the "Talent Managers Association" and usually represent fewer clients than agents (although some have hundreds), therefore they can spend more time on developing actors by helping to prepare them and their marketing materials for working at a professional level. A good manager will come with you to your film festival premiere, go through thousands of headshots with you, look through all of your demo reel footage to find the right one to submit to casting or post online. They will recommend photographers, classes, clothing for auditions, and even whether or not you should have carrots with your mac and cheese for dinner. A good manager picks up the phone, talks to you, knows your type, knows what you want out of your career. A good manager may also work with different agencies and can refer you to an agent (a great way to get an agent).

I know wonderful, boutique agencies where the agents act as managers and speak to their clients every week, who hustle like nobody else and are huge advocates for their actors. Again, they are working to push you without taking a dime. It's all about finding the right one for you.

No matter what, never stop hustling. Too many actors start out working their asses off, then start freelancing with an agent and immediately stop hustling, then they get frustrated when they aren't getting auditions. Actors need to always be working, studying, getting better, staying sharp, and preparing themselves for when that first audition comes in. Remember, your mantra is, "Be the hardest working actor in the room." No excuses.

How do you get an agent or manager? A referral from a casting director who adores you and wants to call on your behalf is the best way. How do you get that? It's who you know. Maybe you've had an agent before and you left on good terms (always) and they can refer you (it happens), or you've booked a couple of jobs through that casting director and you feel comfortable enough to reach out. Not stalk, bother, or harass (or send postcards every other day telling them what you are eating for dinner). It's not a bad idea to reach out to that casting director who loves you and ask if there are any agents *they* recommend. Even better, tell them your situation and let them offer. Second best is a referral from an actor friend who wants to introduce you to their agent. Actors can get weird with this stuff because it could be a conflict of interest, as they could introduce you to their reps and suddenly you are getting more auditions than they are. If you are friends with an actor and they have never seen your work, how can they refer you? That's where joining an acting studio can help. You can meet actors who see your work every week and can really vouch for you. Then again, you may be lucky enough to book a job from all of your hustling skills and you meet an actor on set who wants to refer you to their agent (holla!).

Do good work and the right agent will find you. Know your pitch. If you aren't doing something to sell your talent, how are they going to be able to pitch you to casting?

Another way to find an agent or manager is pay-to-meet workshops ($11,000), where you can just keep stalking them until they fall in love with you. Be careful and do your research. Or finally, you can try to get one by blindly submitting to email addresses you find on IMDBPro and blasting your way through the agent directory praying you caught someone at a moment where they respond to your pic on their screen. That rarely happens. But be ready! I know an actor who sent her headshot and resume out to tons of agents, and one agent responded and asked her to send in her reel. She replied, "Well, it's not quite done yet." And that was it. He passed on her, and she lost her chance.

It might take you going through a few different agents in your career to find the one who really gets you, who loves you, who fights for you. They might not be the biggest, but they always go to bat for you, always push you, and are fiercely loyal. That's who you want. It might take you finding an agent in a different market and finding a way to be a local hire for the shows that film there.

For actors who already have agents, it's all about trust and being open and honest with them. If you are in a signed contract, you need to constantly be making sure your headshots are updated, you have good footage for them to use to be pitching you, and make sure they see you every few months. Stay on their minds by letting them know you are studying with the best, working on-camera every week, taking some specific casting director classes (who are casting shows you are right for) and sharpening your audition skills, blowing them away with your self-tapes and always being ready for game day. If you aren't getting what you want, or it's been slow, you need to sit down and have an honest conversation. If you need to leave and go elsewhere, then be honest with them. If you need to add a manager to the team, then run it by them. They work for you. It's your career. Stop apologizing and ask them for what you need. Like any good relationship, if needs aren't being met, then find someone else. It's not personal, it's business. I don't care if they came to your wedding. You are trying to be a professional actor and you need someone who sees you, understands you, gets you, and can fight for you.

If you are freelancing, and in that weird "trial" phase, make sure the agents you are working with are getting your new headshots and updated footage and you are touching base with them and telling them you are taking a new amazing on-camera class. Let them know you are meeting some casting directors here and there, and that you are very excited about the next steps. It could be that one agent that you haven't gotten an audition from in a year that gets you that one audition that you nail. Then everything changes.

Be prepared for when that opportunity presents itself. Always be ready.

Chapter 9: No Pay, No Meal, No Credit, No Fun
Your Demo Reel Footage

My first demo reel had a montage at the beginning set to a song from "Pulp Fiction." I was badass and clueless and didn't know my type. My reel included a student film from Vassar College (I sucked), and a scene from my sweet industrial film "The Road to Glory, the Path to Addiction" (where I played a nice guy addicted to cocaine and I had to snort baking powder for the whole shoot). Look out De Niro! Needless to say, people told me I needed to get better footage, where the production value was good and it matched the roles I was going to actually play.

In a *dream* world, you have this amazing demo reel showcasing all of the huge roles you booked on TV shows and big-budget films, with you acting opposite very famous actors. In the *real* world, you are desperately trying to cobble together under-exposed student film footage from the *Untitled Goth Project* you did for free (with partial nudity) to find something that might occasionally come across as good acting.

There are a few schools of thought here. If you don't have good, solid, network level, high production value footage, you can either pay to have a "fake scene" made or you can post an "audition style" scene online. Meaning, you can pay hundreds of dollars to have a short scene written for you based on your type, filmed with great equipment, on location, featuring mostly you (you paid for it) in closeup, which might trick some people into thinking it's from a real job. But if your acting is not strong, it still shows, and works against you. And if your scene partner's acting isn't strong, it also works against you.

OR you can find a perfect scene for yourself (online, from a coach, or transcribe one from a TV show), that represents your type, is short and sweet, and film it professionally in front of a neutral backdrop "audition style." Instead of being on location, you (and the viewer) are imagining you are. If you do this well, it won't matter either way. If you don't have footage some agencies are now asking for these self-tapes to use when pitching their clients. Make them perfect.

41

In my mind, it doesn't matter what kind of footage you have, and I know casting directors who strongly agree. At the end of the day, people are probably only watching about ten seconds of your footage. As a director, I don't care if those ten seconds are you sitting in front of a gray wall doing a scene from *Blue Bloods* (as Tom Selleck with a fake mustache) or if you are in what looks like an Applebee's serving up 'derves telling the detectives where the perp is.

You can tell if someone is a good actor in the first few lines.

Yes, the scene needs to look good, and you need to look good in it, and you need to connect and know what you are selling (ew), but I highly recommend you save a few hundred or a few thousand dollars and go for simple first. No matter what, both of these scenarios are placeholders until you get stronger (i.e. big-budget TV) footage to replace it with. So, spend your money wisely (see the next chapter on pay-to-meet workshops).

Here's what happens when casting a project. This is from my experience of scrolling through thousands of headshots online when casting my first three films. You have about 1000 submissions per role and have to whittle it down to one. Obviously, you can't see every person who submits (wouldn't that be great?).

Right off the bat, you knock out everyone who isn't the right "type" for the part (too old, too thin, too creepy, looks like grandma). As I said before, the next step is clicking on "Slate." Then you can click on "Media" (if you don't have media, you aren't even being considered in my opinion). *This* is where you upload that short little scene that I just told you about. At this point, I'm like, "I like the headshot, I like their look and the way they sound, and oh my god, they are also a good actor," because you can tell good acting right off the bat.

Now we request a self-tape to see what they do with the material, and how they interpret it. This is where the all-important self-tape skills come in handy, as it is a *deal closer*. I want to know their *essence*, their *vibe*. This is where you want to show them how serious you are, as I have requested self-tapes from 100 of the 1000 submissions (per role). Already some people didn't even submit a tape (idiots), so I can knock them out.

Now we want the actors who are *ready to play ball*, are camera ready, are memorized and making choices. They are *likable* and someone I may want to work with and are ready to step onto set. I will scroll through all the videos on my phone whenever I have time, earmark the ones I like, watch them over several days, revisit some again and again, all before I have even met the actors in person. Then, I will bring in 20 actors in total, all of whose work I am fiercely familiar with. At this point, I will want to work with each actor to see how *adaptable* they are, how easily they can take direction, and hear their take on the character. I may also have them read something else (a cold-read).

Let's be clear. There isn't time to sit around and watch every actor's reel who submits for projects. That would take months, and I'd rather watch the *Kardashians*. So, in your footage, you *have* to grab the attention of the viewer within ten seconds (same goes for auditions), have it look and sound good, have a strong moment before, and make us believe that you're really in that situation. Make it great. Kill it.

A typical reel should be no more than 90 seconds (again, most decisions are made after 10). Piece together a bunch of clips around 10-20 seconds each. Some agents prefer individual clips instead of a full reel now. This way, when casting posts a breakdown for a role, they can send the clip that closely matches that role, to give you a better chance of getting seen. So, the footage needs to sell your type! If they ask for a clip of you playing a high-powered lawyer, maybe don't send the depressed drug addict scene you did in acting class? Keep the footage current, make it look good, and make sure it has high production value. Most importantly, make sure it focuses on *you*. Do you know how many people have footage where it features the other person in the scene? You are making it so much harder for casting and harder for yourself.

Chapter 10: Speed Dating
Pay-to-Meet Workshops

The one and only time I took a casting director class was right out of Vassar College. I signed up for a four week "How to Audition for TV" workshop with a well-known casting director who casts for a major network (I didn't know who she was at the time so nerves weren't an issue). Over four weeks, she got to know me and I got to know her. To me, it was just a class I could rehearse in, as I recently got an agent who was getting me big auditions, and I was a dude with a theatre degree who didn't know his way around a camera frame. On week one I bombed! I mean, bad. She assigned me sides from a WB show and I did some serious Shakespeare style acting. Imagine if the class was only one night and cost me $80. You think she'd bring me into her office? Nope! However, I had three more weeks. On week 2, I brought in the sides for one of my upcoming auditions for a show called "Strangers with Candy" (yeah, the one I mentioned earlier). The character was blind, and I launched into the whole scene staring at the reader's shirt. When I finished, she asked why I didn't look the reader in the eye. I mentioned the whole blind thing. Her feedback: "Well, it was weird, but I think it worked." I didn't push, I didn't bring in a blind stick. I just got into character. And I booked it. And week after week I learned how not to overact on camera, and every week after class I sat in front of my VCR and watched my class footage, seeing for myself what worked and didn't work in the frame. And I still have the VHS tape at home to prove it. She helped me with my TV and film audition technique, and she saw my work over time.

As I write this, there are endless options out there for actors everywhere to (pay to audition) get an education on the casting process. There are online classes, and in-person one on ones and group workshops taught by casting directors (more likely, associates or assistants), agents, managers, and also my uncle and next-door neighbor Billy (tell him I said hi and to give me my headshots back). Everyone's a teacher now, and these "opportunities" are major cash cows, geared towards actors who are "investing" in their careers. It's who you know, right? Well, *I know* a girl who spent $11,000 on them. In a year. And hasn't been called in once.

And she is young and insanely talented. I think it's really important to do some soul searching here, and as the emails and credits and discount codes are bogarting your inbox on a daily basis, and the promises of stardom are dangled in front of you, take a step back and ask yourself if it's the right move for you. Paying money to do a two-minute scene in front of someone one time is not something I have ever done, nor has any successful working actor I have known.

In my opinion, there is a time and a place for these. There are casting directors who your hard-working managers are submitting you to, who simply won't call you in. Perhaps there's a world where an actor *who is ready* pays a small fee to get in front of that casting person and shows them how good you are over a couple of weeks. In that time, they see that you take direction and are able to tackle different types of characters. Then perhaps next time there is a role *they are casting,* and you are submitted by *your trusted rep*, then *the stars collide,* and they bring you in. Everything else feels like a giant waste of money and actors need to spend money wisely. Headshots, video footage, casting websites, training, and creating your own work. Eleven thousand dollars is enough to fund an entire short film or even an entire season of a web series. See where I'm going here?

Sometimes casting directors, agents and managers are there to get a paycheck. Remember many of them are freelancing too and these workshops supplement their income in between jobs. Some of them actually give *wonderful* tips and feedback over the course of a 2-4 week class that are tremendously helpful to actors. *Sometimes* they meet actors they are excited about. *Usually,* the best-case result is an audition for a one-line co-star or possibly freelancing with a rep. Best case. And how many times do you need to pay before someone knows your work? 5? 10? So, you are spending about $500 for a fan? Nah. Buy a fan at Home Depot. It's cheaper (too soon?).

In 2009, Los Angeles introduced the Krekorian Talent Scam Prevention Act, which basically said workshops can't charge actors for an audition for a potential job opportunity, and therefore casting directors, agents and managers aren't allowed to take headshots and resumes after the class. Some casting directors who did workshops out there violated this and were busted, and the workshop facilities closed. This law does not exist in New York, but the idea is that other cities will follow. Stay tuned. Some places in New York have already stopped taking headshots.

Advice for new actors

Yes, actors should invest in their careers, and many will think of pay-to-meet workshops as an investment. However, a lot of actors are signing up for these *before they are ready*. There is no "fast track." They are meeting decision-makers, learning about what they like in the audition room, and they don't even know how to act. They've never even learned their craft. Going to too many of these will kill an actor's creativity, and instead of growing as an actor, they are being taught "don't do that." If you hear that enough, you will be an uninteresting shell of an actor who has an extensive list of all of the casting offices in town and what their pet peeves are. Good for you. Have you gotten any auditions?

Remember you are an artist first, right? Make sure you are *good* and *hirable* before you throw your hard-earned bartending/dog-walking money at these. It's better for newer actors to focus on building a kickass resume, gaining confidence in their skills, creating amazing footage, and learning how to audition in a safe environment before they get in front of the big wigs. Actors need to be in a safe class to learn, grow and figure out their type. They need to discover what types of roles they would and would not play and work outside of their comfort zone. It's the only way to get better.

If you want to be smart about it, and specific, and invest your money wisely, do this: research the casting directors, agents and managers you are thinking about meeting. Look at CastingAbout, which is an amazing website that will tell you who is casting what and when. Look at the bios and rosters on IMDBPro, see who the agents and managers represent. Do they already have three of your type? Then why do they need another? Are they casting a show that hires people like you? Or is it totally against your type? Are they currently casting or on hiatus? Ask yourself the tough questions before you part with your hard-earned money.

Be smart with your money. Be good to yourself.

Chapter 11: I Play Psychopaths
Your Actor "Type"

At my very first headshot session when I was 22, the headshot photographer sat me down and we discussed my type for two hours, all the roles I wanted to play, etc. He said: "Beer commercials," I said: "Shakespeare." He made me wear a ripped-up Abercrombie military hat in half the photos, and in the other half, I wore a shirt with a stretched-out collar and was rocking some major razor burn (I had just started shaving at age 21). I think my hair was parted down the middle. So, the only "type" I could grab onto was "nerd with weird hat." Get in line, ladies.

Your actor "type" describes the kinds of roles you will be playing when you first start out or for all of your life. Type is what people see you as the second you walk into the room, before you start actually "acting". It's something that is very close to who you actually are, your *essence,* but doesn't define you. It's not personal, it's just how people in the casting world see you. As a type. They need to fit you into a breakdown. Sometimes a breakdown will read, "We need a Shailene Woodley type." Sure, a lot of people could *try* to do that, get coached on it, and work really hard to reach that, but there are other people who just naturally fit that type.

Examples of some types: high school popular girl, middle school loner, soccer mom, upper east side woman, creepy thug (me), jock, high powered young lawyer, nerdy friend (with weird hat), sketchy character type, sexy-serial killer, fun-chubby best friend, cool dad, hipster, farmer, deadbeat dad. Don't obsess, don't get locked in, just be honest with yourself.

At the beginning of your professional career, you will get hired to play parts that are close to who you are. When you fight your type, you won't get hired. Own it. Say yes to everything. Then, later in your career, you can make a decision to actively change your type, but it may actually change naturally. You don't want to say you are a sophisticated upper east side woman if you recently shaved your head and tattooed your roommate's name on it. Get it? Don't force your type on people. See how you get hired. See how the market perceives you. Look at the roles you are booking.

When you watch TV, notice what shows are hiring people that look like you. Look those actors up on IMDBPro. Educate yourself. Find your niche. What show are you right for? What actors are you most similar to? What agency represents them? What else have they booked? "Type" used to matter more, as network execs only hired certain types on TV. Now, because of the huge diversity push in television, there are so many types on TV these days, on so many different networks, which means there is a place for everyone. Some might say they aren't even hiring "types" anymore, they are hiring "people". Just be you. The hardest working version of you.

Chapter 12: Hit Me Up on Insta
The Importance of Social Media

Everyone wants to be famous, but they do not want to do the work. It's not sustainable. I always think of the Thomas Edison quote, "Success is 1% inspiration and 99% perspiration." The work gets you there. You might have a lot of followers and suddenly be given a great opportunity, but if you don't have craft, you are screwed. Once I ran into a castoff from the reality show "Survivor" at an audition for a huge new CBS pilot. I asked him where he studied, and he said, "There were a lot of cameras following us around on the show, so I'm pretty comfortable with them now." Cool brah. I think I saw him serving crudités to AG dolls the other day.

There's a lot to be said here, but let's keep it simple. You are either a social media person or you are not. I know a casting director who had to cast five leads in a film, and two out of the five had to have at least 60,000 followers on social media, according to their contract from the producers. I know another casting director who cast his entire film from Instagram, because he was looking for "real musicians" who had a following. It wasn't *their* decision, it was the director's or producer's. Whatever, it's gonna happen. Before you get mad about it, understand this: more than ever, it's very hard to get people to watch your independent feature film, unless you have stars in it. The word "star" has become broader in context, and includes not only actors but influencers, the idea being that if they post about their next film, chances are a percentage of their followers will come to see it. It's all about eyes and ticket sales, even if it means they aren't as good of an actor. Dwayne Johnson ("The Rock") has a huge social media following, therefore commanding a hefty paycheck. He knows the influence he has over ticket sales to movies he stars in. Smart, smart man. And he backs it up with his craft.

Do you need to go out and start being active on social media and hash-tagging the hell out of every food post? No. But I have found that social media is a great way to network with other actors, directors, producers, and filmmakers that you meet naturally, at either auditions, or film festivals, and it keeps you fresh on their minds when they are working on their next project. I think it's important to naturally and organically engage with them on social media, without being desperate ("bring me in, please"). Desperation reeks from a mile away.

Agencies are now opening divisions to represent influencers. They are seeing social media as a way to generate revenue, and also for potentially building a crossover career in television and film. That dude from *Young Sheldon* was discovered from his movie review videos on YouTube! People can now sit in their living room, post interesting (or stupid) videos, gain followers, and potentially get a collaboration deal with a brand, possibly an agent to represent them, and possibly some bigger opportunities. But when that day comes, they must know what they are doing. So do the work first, be a great actor, know your craft, then gain that following organically.

Advice

- If you are on social media, here are some dos and don'ts.

- As excited as you are when you book a job, never, ever post the name of the product or television show online. Actors have gotten fired over this. Imagine you book this great job, and you are so excited that you blast it out on your "actor newsletter" saying "Guess who's booking!" and then you lose the job. All that hard work down the drain.

- Never post a selfie on set, unless you have asked the appropriate person. Now actors have to sign a contract when they book a job that says they won't take any pictures on set. Or the call sheet says, "No photography and social media posting during the shoot."

- Never post a picture with an audition script in it. Spoilers!

- Never pay for followers or likes. It's lame and desperate.

- Don't "friend request" a casting director. I feel like every casting director everywhere must have thousands of "pending friend requests" from actors.

- Avoid political statements. It could literally cost you the job.

- Every kid's account should be managed by a parent (and say it on their profile). There are just too many creepers out there.

- Casting directors look at your social media. Don't post pictures of you partying. Or inappropriate pics. Nothing says "wholesome dad" like you chugging a beer at Hooters.

- Don't be weird.

Chapter 13: Get Off Your Ass
A Guide to Creating Your Own Work

One of my adult students had an agent, but was never getting auditions, and wasn't happy about it. She is a funny, talented, unique type, that people weren't hiring. She had this idea to write something for herself, about the world of actors who get hired to run "Princess Parties" for kids. She did this for a living and had some hilarious stories. She knew this world well and thought it was really funny, but didn't know where to start. She took a workshop with me, then set off to write it, crowdfund it, and film it. It is the single best piece of acting I've ever seen her do, and she has since won awards for Best Screenplay, Best Actress, and Best Comedy, and is happier than I've ever seen her. Now, they are knocking on her door.

I work with actors every day, and so many of them have talent you wouldn't believe. They are at the top of their game, but extremely frustrated that it doesn't translate to becoming a working actor. I get it. They will say to me: "I know I am good, so what am I doing wrong? Should I look for a different agent? I just want to be going out for co-star roles." And here is what I say every time: "Instead of worrying about getting one line on TV, why don't you make something yourself, a role that only you can do, and gear it towards your strengths?" And they say, "I wouldn't even know where to begin" or "Sounds like a lot of work" or "I'm not a writer."

Original content is everything.

One of the most important things an actor can do is create opportunities for themselves. Too many actors sit around waiting for the phone to ring, taking workshops, and complaining that more isn't happening. They are mad at their agents and wondering why they don't have more auditions. Idle time is dangerous. The demons creep in and eat your soul.

When I wrote my first film, I downloaded free screenwriting software (Celtx) and spent two weeks writing a little bit every day. Then I had some friends read it. Then I decided to see if I could raise some money. Then I found a crew. Then I filmed for a week in the backyard where I grew up. Then I went to 8 film festivals with it, had red carpet premieres, and rented out the Anthology Archives in New York and invited all my students. Why?

To show my acting students how easy it is.

Let's talk about Phoebe Waller-Bridge, the star of *Fleabag*. Phoebe was a somewhat unknown actor with some BBC credits under her belt, who went and created a one-woman show based on this character she had envisioned. She wrote it for herself, focused on her art, and people found her. Now it's streaming on Amazon Prime and she has three Emmys and, as of 2020, a Golden Globe. With newer platforms like Netflix, Amazon, and Hulu, there is more flexibility. It's not about box office anymore, so there is room for new, exciting, original content from less bankable stars.

I am a firm believer that actors always need to be inspired and to be taking steps to stay fulfilled creatively, or else they will lose their way and forget why they pursued this in the first place. Every actor will tell you how good they are, but very few are actually *doing something* to show that. They might be in a class, or have an audition here and there, or they are constantly submitting themselves for projects, but other than that, they are rarely pursuing outlets to push them creatively. They spend very little time actually *acting*.

This needs to change. Actors need to train, to get better, to create opportunities for *themselves*, to hire *themselves* for projects, and not sit around wondering why they aren't getting submitted for that one line on *Madam Secretary* (too soon?). Let me tell you something: you can take all the casting workshops in the world, meet all the casting directors in town, work your "type" scene 1000 different ways, finally get called in, book a one-line role on a show, film for one hour, put it on your resume, get paid $1000, and pray to god your part isn't cut before airing. The whole process, while it's cool to tell mom and dad that you are on a TV show that people actually watch, will leave you feeling empty. These are throwaway roles, and you rarely get any feedback when you are filming, and you go home and think to yourself "That's it? That's what actors are desperate to get?"

You are better than that. You are a trained actor who is capable of doing some pretty damn incredible work. Shoot higher. I'm not saying that booking a co-star is a disappointment. Not at all. It's amazing. You won the lottery. You did it. You got the agent, the callback and the role. This is how people start their careers, with that first booking that gets your foot in the door and puts you in the club. I just want you to hold yourself to a higher standard, to shoot for bigger roles, and to not settle. Don't be a co-star actor for the rest of your life.

Let me tell you something about creating your own work. It's the most satisfying, frustrating, inspiring way to gain perspective in this business. It will make you a better actor and will help you understand what really matters. When you create your own work, you build a universe, and you realize that actors are but a small part of that universe, a small and necessary part of a bigger picture. From working with an idea in your own head, to putting it down on the page, to casting, to watching self-tapes, having callbacks, to hiring a crew to bring your dream to life, the experience makes you understand that it's all bigger than you. When you understand this, you become a better, less desperate actor because you understand you are one of many pieces and that it's not all about you. I'll say that again: it's not all about you.

Don't just act. You can't be dependent on other people to write roles for you. This leads to being very frustrated most of the time that you aren't getting the roles you want. Have a dream role? Write. It. And. Stop. Complaining.

So, the big question is: Why bother? How many people actually get somewhere from writing a short film for themselves?

The answer is…Some? A few? Who cares? Write the role you want to do. Start small, with no budget. Get some good footage. Go to some festivals and meet people. It feeds your soul, and maybe, just maybe, another door opens. And you are doing something inspiring called *talent stacking*. You are learning all sides of filmmaking.

It doesn't need to be about getting on TV. It should be about feeling inspired creatively. If you want to play the game, spend $11,000 on workshops, learn the pet peeves of every casting office in town, write it down in an Excel spreadsheet, and be the "smartest auditioner in the room," then that's your lane. And it's a small one with a possible dead-end (oof). I don't know about you, but I would want to be in a lane that could go somewhere. I want to help draw the damn map.

But if you want to make something from the ground up, stay inspired, and be working on a project every minute of every day, learning all the ins and outs of what goes into filmmaking, all the conference calls, look books, scriptwriting, and creating a project out of thin air, that you get to see on a big screen in front of other filmmakers in different cities, then please, please, please do that. I highly recommend it. Don't do it because you want to ultimately have a nice little YouTube link to send out blindly to agents. Don't do it because you hope a casting director sees it. Do it because you want to take charge of your career, do something other actors are afraid of, take a risk, and use every ounce of your creativity and put it into something you are proud of from start to finish.

Are you with me? Let's go through it step by step. If you are still feeling lazy, skip to my chapter "Don't be a lazy ass."

STEP ONE: Write it

Download free screenwriting software (I recommend Celtx). Focus on something short. Ten pages is a good length (works out to about ten minutes). This can be a web-series or short film. Don't worry about structure, you just want a few scenes and a clear journey. Focus on a small idea and make it *personal*. Keep it simple, honest, and real. Give yourself a week to write it, which is about a few pages a day. Let it suck. Don't censor yourself. Write it all out. Instead of sitting around submitting for free student films on Actors Access (no pay, some meals, maybe credit), or thinking about writing an email to your agent and firing them, take a few minutes each morning and write (or jot notes on your phone on the subway and throughout the day). What about? Write what you know. Who's the character that only you could play? Write it in *your* voice. Then go back and cut out all the excess. Most new writers overwrite the scenes, give too much scene description, and don't personalize the work. Make it personal. Make it real. Move the needle. Say what you want to say. Write the role you have been dying to play.

STEP TWO: Budget it

You've written a script, and you kind of like it. How do you even know what this is gonna cost? Are you shooting it for free with equipment you already have, and friends who are willing to work for free? If not, you will need to come up with a budget.

The most effective, affordable approach is to write a script with only two characters (keeps the amount of shots down), using all interiors (so you don't have to worry about the sun going down or renting a lighting package at night), at a location you have access to (your apartment or your roommate's pool house). This will keep the budget down. At this point, you want to hire a *line producer* for a couple hundred bucks (or a friend), who can go through the script and give you a line by line estimated budget for what it would cost to make it.

They will ask you things like:

Is it SAG-AFTRA? You only need to do this if you want to use at least one union actor. I recommend avoiding this in your first project, as it requires paperwork, timesheets, budget reports, and paying into that actor's pension and health. But if you want to hire your friend who is a famous actor, then it's worth it.

Are you paying your actors? I think all actors should be paid. Even $50 a day helps them get out of bed to work for 12-14 hours on your passion project. It's like asking someone to help you move. At least buy them lunch, right?

Are you hiring a casting director? If you want access to top tier actors, and have the breakdown posted on Breakdown Services for every agent and manager to see, then pay a casting director to set up a two-day casting session for you. If you are going to use your friends, don't even worry about it. If you want to see lots of actors who don't necessarily have representation, and who are looking for work, then post on Actors Access.

Are you renting any camera or lighting packages? This can get expensive, as you rent cameras and lenses by the day, as well as lights. However, if you film it all inside during the day, with cameras you already own (maybe your friend owns a fancy camera), then you can avoid huge expenses here. When you rent cameras, you usually have to prove that you have production insurance, in case you break one of the fancy cameras on set. So, this cost adds up.

What about sound? You can't skimp on this. Sound is one of the most important elements of any project. A good project with bad sound is unwatchable. Spend the money here. I've spent up to $600 per day to have a professional sound person who has their own equipment. It matters! Want to get a better deal? Ask someone to work on a weekend for two days, between their higher-paying jobs. Negotiate! Be a producer!

Will you have an AD? An Assistant Director will schedule the shoot, decide how much time each scene will need, and will make sure you get through it. This will cost a few hundred per day if you decide to go this route.

At the end of the day, the most money you will spend will be on post-production costs—editing, color correction, sound mixing, sound design, and festival submissions.

Editor

Are you editing it yourself? You are either editing this in iMovie or Final Cut Pro, you are good with Adobe Premiere Pro, or you are hiring a professional editor who will charge you by the hour or will offer a flat rate for the project. For a short film, an editor might charge $1500 for a flat rate, or $80 an hour. It all depends on who you find, and if they are willing to take a pay cut to help with your passion project. You are developing relationships, and most likely will be working with a lot of these people again. Everyone knows someone else. Be nice and respectful, and they will work with you on the next 10 projects. Be a dick and they will butcher your sound in post.

Colorist

You need someone to color correct your film. Always. A good colorist might charge you $500 or more to go through your film, fix color mistakes, create mood, match the color of faces in each shot, etc. It's very important. If one frame looks dark, and the next one light, and it's supposed to be the same scene, your film will look amateur.

Sound Designer

Maybe your friend wrote an original song for the film. Maybe you want to add an instrumental track behind it. Maybe you want to add atmospheric sounds (birds, room tone, etc.). The sound designer will put this together for you.

Sound Mixer

This is where all of the elements are mixed together (dialogue, foley, sound effects, background, music) and timed out with picture. Do it right, as this makes a huge difference when you see it on a big screen at a festival with huge speakers.

Festival Fees

Festival budget. If you want this to be seen at all, you are going to want to save some money for festival submissions. By looking on the main film submission website Filmfreeway.com you can find almost all of the film festivals in the world (some only allow you to submit through their own website). Plan to spend between $25 and $50 per submission (some offer bulk discounts, early-bird discounts, waiver codes, etc.). Do your research, ask your friends, and try to find out which festivals are worth your time. Look at the kind of films they have programmed in the past. You probably want to submit to between 10 and 20 festivals in total. It's like applying to college. You have your long shots, your top choices, and your safeties. Some festivals are just a glorified screening in a small room with very little promotion, and some go all out with social media, award shows, networking, filmmaker lunches, happy hours, and are just really fun. I've been to dozens of film festivals for my films, and at some of them I've met people who became my lifelong friends. I went to one where I was the only one in the audience for my short film. I gave myself a standing ovation, because I spent two years working on it. Holla!

STEP 3: Finance it

You could shoot the entire project with equipment you already have (the movie *Tangerine* was shot entirely on iPhones), in a location that's free, with your actor friends, and give them peanut butter and jelly, and have them wear their own clothes, then edit and color correct it yourself (or have a friend do it for the credit), and only pay festival fees (about $25-$50 a pop for a short).

You could also go the investor route and see if a family member will give you some money towards it. Maybe your rich aunt just wants to support your dream and is willing to give you $10,000, knowing full well that films don't make money and she won't see that money back. This could make for a very awkward Thanksgiving.

Or you could raise the entire amount through crowdfunding platforms (what I did) like Indiegogo, Seed & Spark, Kickstarter, or even GoFundMe. I've done four short films, and each one was budgeted at about $15,000. I ain't paying my hard-earned money for that shit. I created a fun little campaign video, offered cool perks, initiated a 30-day campaign, asking for anything from $10 (social media shout-out), to $1000 (producer credit and set visit). You'd be surprised at how many people want to help you get your film made. Every dollar goes towards bringing your passion project to life and making the best film you can make.

And guess what? You might only raise $1000, in which case, you are going to have to call in some favors, make some sacrifices, negotiate and barter, but that is what will make you a great producer, and give you a greater understanding of how crazy filmmaking is. You will be wearing many different hats, doing 15 different jobs, and the acting part, while important, is just a small part of it. Remember: it's not about you.

STEP 4: Production and post-production

This is the most exciting part of it: when someone says, "Action" and you suddenly have a crew, are actually filming the script YOU wrote, and are probably also STARRING IN. Whether it's a one-day shoot, or five days, you are living the dream. You are obsessing over your schedule, your locations, your actors, and you are making sure you get all the shots from your "shot list" so that you have all the ingredients to give the editor after you are done shooting. The editor will play with different takes and come up with an "assembly" cut, which is a linear cut of the film in the order of shots originally intended in the script. It won't have music, sound design or color correction, and you will think it sucks. It doesn't. You will then do a "fine cut" with the editor, and get down to the tiny reactions you want, the important cutaways, the transitions and you will ultimately make this film interesting, and tell the story only YOU want to tell. After you "lock the edit," you will send it off simultaneously to a composer, as well as a colorist. Once the film has those two elements, you will send to a sound mixer, who will mix the dialogue, music, and effects into one file with all of the elements. This is where you will really see your film for the first time, and it might blow you away. Then your editor will match that to picture, and spit out several versions of the film, which can then be submitted to festivals.

STEP 5: Submit to festivals

Here is my advice. Don't submit to every festival under the sun. It's expensive. What niche is your film? Horror? Experimental? LGBT? Drama? Spec pilot? Submit to local festivals that you will actually go to so that you can network. Decide if you want to send to first-tier festivals (Sundance and SXSW), second-tier festivals, or third-tier festivals. Some of these festivals require that your film premieres there, so read the submission qualifications carefully. Come up with a list of reaches and safeties. There are tons in New York, both big and small. Ask around. It's an incredible feeling when you get into one. You can invite your friends to the screening, and you can network, meet cool people, see other films, and learn what filmmaking is all about. And sometimes you win awards! Here is some advice on submitting from Adirondack Film Festival Artistic Director Chad Rabinowitz: *"I can point to one thing everyone SHOULD do. That's 'Tell us what makes your story unique and do it succinctly.' After programming so many shows, I'm always looking to give my audience a new experience or to show them a character, an event, or a tale they haven't seen before. But if you can't explain it in 3 sentences, then I can't sell it in 1 (which is generally all I have when making an ad). So find a way to hook me in with as few sentences as possible and I'll be more likely to go into your work excited about the material and looking for ways to put it into my festival."*

STEP 6: Sell it

These days it's so much easier to get your short film seen and have it land on a major streaming platform like Amazon Prime, iTunes, Hulu, Tubi TV, Amazon Worldwide, and some allow you to distribute it yourself and decide your price point. You won't make much, but guess what? You can tell everyone you know to watch this cool project you spent a year working on. And all they have to do is turn on their TV to see it. It's awesome.

You will understand the joy and frustration of filmmaking on a whole other level, and will gain perspective, confidence, and intelligence. You are not just an actor, but a writer, director, producer, editor, and you are doing something essential called *talent stacking*. This is where you are learning all parts of filmmaking (basically putting yourself through film school boot camp), and you will be able to up the ante on your next project you create, which will have a bigger budget, better crew, and you will have already learned what *not* to do. Then suddenly you are getting accepted into festivals, possibly winning some Best Picture laurels, meeting other actors and filmmakers who say, "We should collaborate," and you are doing it because you love it and it's fun. And agents who passed on you as an actor are now pitching their clients to you as a filmmaker (happened to me). As Mark Duplass famously said in his SXSW Keynote speech, *"At the point the cavalry actually shows up, you probably are the cavalry. Go make films."*

And this whole time you've been experiencing the filmmaking process, you have tasted something that's career-changing and you want to do it all over again. You aren't focusing on the fact that you aren't getting in the room for whatever reason. You are too busy to worry and too excited about your project to care. Now you want to make a feature! Or now you want to make several more episodes and post it as a web-series to see how much traction it gets, because you have a unique voice that nobody has seen or heard before, you have something to say, and a unique way of saying it. Because new, original content is everything these days. You aren't just a utility player (co-star) who is told where to stand and what to say. You are hiring other actors. You are in charge of going through the 4,000 submissions, all the little headshot jpegs, the cutesy little "slate shots," the media, bad footage, good footage, self-tapes, and deciding who you want to have in *your* project. You are a better actor now because you are actually *acting*. You are a better auditioner because you helped cast your first film and have a deeper understanding of the casting process.

And then, your agent calls you for an audition (because that's oddly how it works).

So, stop waiting around for stuff to happen, stop being stagnant, stop paying and forcing decision-makers to meet you, stop complaining about your agents and lack of auditions, and start creating projects you are proud of. Invite your friends and family to a film festival where your movie is up on the big screen, and as the opening credits start, you see: "Written by," "Starring" or "Directed by" and your name pops up. Trust me, you just fed your soul.

Chapter 14: Brand Spanking New
Advice for Newbies Young and Old

When I started out, I did community theatre. I was Friedrich in "Sound of Music" at Amarante's Dinner Theatre in New Haven, performed in the round, for old people who could barely hear my voice dropping the octave halfway through "My Favorite Things" (it gets high). But I made money (nickels), and I felt famous. I learned what worked and what didn't work, and how to be around actors at a higher level than me. I also learned I needed a voice coach. I could not for the life of me hit that High G in "So Long Farewell." After college (and about 30 plays later), I moved to New York and sent out my headshot and cover letter to every casting director in LA, saying I would "fly myself out for extra work." Good god, I was desperate. I did everything wrong, but my god, I wanted it, and I wanted to make money doing it. I had trained for four years in school, done dozens of plays, taken classes, worked on my technique, and felt like I had a good sense of my ability. But I didn't have a good sense of the industry. That took time, but I wanted to work professionally.

It doesn't matter how old you are. I work with actors who are 5 years old, and actors who are 80. There is a place for everyone (commercials, community theatre, voiceovers, TV, film, regional theatre, industrials). The real question you have to ask yourself is whether you want to move to a major market and try to break in at a *professional* level, or whether you want to stay where you are, do it as a hobby, do *Death of a Salesman* scenes in your living room with your roommate, or slowly build your resume (and confidence) before making the move later.

Some people want to do this for *fun*, and just want to act, in whatever capacity, and don't really care who sees them doing it. For those people, I say go for it. Stay where you are, do anything and everything you can within a 100-mile radius of your town. Take classes, audition, do readings, get your friends together and make films, run scenes, find an artistic community, and get better. Be a big fish in your small town. Do everything you can to build your skill set, much like an athlete or a dancer.

Stretch yourself and get out of your comfort zone. Make art. Not everyone gets to do it for money or gets to do it professionally in a major market. Do it because it's a hobby and you love it. Other people do sports. You *act*.

Say you want to go bigger. Unless you live on Pepperidge Farm, chances are you are in or *near* a city that offers a chance to pursue acting, even on a local level. There are casting directors in some of these cities. Audition for theatre, regional commercials, put on a show with your friends, do readings, take classes, do anything and everything you can and just say yes. Get in front of an audience. Entertain. Learn. Develop confidence and skills that will cross over into your everyday life.

Say you want to pursue this *professionally* and make money from it. If you actually *live* in a major market like New York, Los Angeles, Atlanta, Austin, or New Orleans (there are others), then get a great headshot (not a JC Penny glamour shot), take an on-camera class, sign up for Actors Access, put up some footage, and submit yourself for any and all short films and student films. You may not get paid money, but you will get experience. Experience breeds confidence. Confidence and skill lead to work. In a major television and film market, where there is a lot of production happening, there are a lot of high-profile roles that need to be cast. Yes, you need an agent to get access to these roles. All of these cities have productions coming through (because of strong tax incentives, which are always changing), as well as casting directors, agents, and managers that have set up shop (as well as thousands of actors). If you are young, this is easier, as it is less about extensive experience, and more about type and whether or not an agent or manager will sign you and send you out for the big stuff. Regardless, you must train with the pros, learn the ins and outs of the business, learn what is being cast and when (CastingAbout.com is a great resource), and decide if you are ready for the rejection and success that comes with auditioning in the big leagues. It's a lot of rejection. You can't be too fragile.

If you want to be competitive, you must get into a class. A good one. Train like an athlete. Take a class that kicks your ass every week. One that puts you in front of a camera, and that simultaneously teaches you how to audition, how to act on-camera, and also how to command the frame. Self-tape yourself every day at home with mock audition sides. Do everything you can to be the best, physically and emotionally. If the idea of going to an audition freaks you out, then work it out in the classroom. Do whatever you have to do to be at the top of your game. Make mistakes. Commit to failure. Get up and grow stronger. Learn the business, research the agents and casting directors out there, know the market inside and out. Go to film festivals, go see great theatre. Network. Understand the hierarchy, learn how to market yourself. Get a great headshot, from a *professional* photographer. Don't spend too much. Format your resume to industry standard (I talk about it in my book *10 Steps to Breaking into Acting*, available on Amazon). Sign up for Actors Access and/or Casting Networks and upload two clips of killer work and a slate shot. Figure out your type. Book a bunch of jobs and learn by being on set, when expectations are low, and nobody is going to see the final product. Prep yourself for the big leagues. Act like a professional and people will treat you like one. Level up.

You will know when you are ready to seek out professional representation, be it an agent or manager. Nothing is better than getting a meeting with an agent, and finally getting an audition for a network show, and finally landing your first speaking role, joining the union, and being part of the club. It's awesome. In the meantime, focus on the work.

Chapter 15: Stage Moms, Inc.
Advice for Kids and Parents

I once tried to do a self-tape for a kid whose mom spent half of our coaching session fixing her daughter's hair (which looked totally fine), and when it finally came time to work on the scene, the girl didn't know her lines. At all. The mom wanted me to feed her the lines while recording. Obviously, that wouldn't be a good idea. So, we couldn't get the tape. I felt bad. And I told her agent that the girl simply wasn't ready. And this was a big agency! And a huge opportunity! I have cute kids too. They love to throw tantrums, throw forks at me, and paint on my walls. It's adorable. It doesn't mean they are actors.

I coach lots of kids and teens, both on auditions, and on-set after they have booked the job. That means I also work with a lot of moms and dads (it's a package deal). I absolutely love working with kids, especially if they love it as much as I do. I've been there when they nail the take and for the tears of joy when they book the job, but I've also been there for the panic attacks, the boredom, the jealousy, the frustration, the fatigue, and the general disinterest. Sometimes they don't care, and they don't want it. And that's ok! Some do it for a few years, and then lose interest when they go to high school or go off to college. Some will do it for the rest of their lives.

Kids read this

You are awesome. You want to be an actor, and you want to audition for big TV shows, films, Broadway, and commercials. You see other kids doing it, and you want to be part of this beautiful world of playing cool characters, working on big sets, and getting to do something you love. And truthfully, it is mind-blowing. When it happens. But even when it happens, it's a lot of work. It's long hours and banking school time while you are on set. And between those jobs, you have to constantly be memorizing scripts, running around to auditions, and maybe going months or years between those jobs. When it's busy, you will be pulled in ten different directions, between acting, sports, school, and all the other things. So you have to *love* it, and not let yourself get burnt out. And don't worry about what jobs other kids are booking. Seriously, who cares? Sometimes you are one inch too tall, or your hair is the wrong color and doesn't match the mother in the show. Everyone has their turn.

If you'd rather hang out with your friends than learn a 10-page script for tomorrow, then be honest with yourself and your parents and your agent or manager. They will understand. If you fight with your mom and dad every time you try to make a self-tape, then go to a professional studio to read it, coach it, and tape it (don't let mom or dad give you line readings please, as that is always very obvious to casting directors). You have to really, really enjoy it, because there will be some great rewards. Sitting down with your friends and watching your episode of that TV show you booked is the most surreal feeling. Seeing yourself on the big screen at the movie theatre is nothing short of incredible. Being in a play on Broadway at a young age is something I never imagined when I was young. Just always make sure you are always, always enjoying the process. Because I never want you to look back and say you missed your childhood stressing about auditions when you could have been hanging out with your friends.

Okay, now listen up. When you break down a script, don't focus on *how* you are saying lines. Focus on *why*. It's not a memorization contest. You should know how you feel about *anything* and *everything* in the scene. How can you make it personal? How can you relate? How can you make it *yours?* Be. Yourself. That is the most interesting quality to a casting director.

And remember, it's not a costume party. Don't roll in with your full *Music Man* costume. Dress to *suggest* the character. Focus on the acting.

69

Parents read this

My advice is this: if it ain't fun for them, then don't do it. This business is crazy, full of lots of work, on top of the stress, rejection, and waiting around. If they'd rather play *Minecraft* or *Smash Bros*, then let them do it. If they just want to act and have fun, then let them do a school play, take an improv class, get together with friends and film a scene with their phones, and learn how to edit it into a cool little movie to show Aunt Becki at Thanksgiving.

If they are doing this at a professional level, there are sacrifices that come with it, but also huge rewards. They might get 10 pages to memorize the night before, have to knock out 3 self-tapes, you may have to take them out of school early, then to an acting coach (because your agent said so), singing coach, dance coach (also maybe therapy?), travel two hours to the city, do 7 great auditions in a day (TV, film, commercial, voiceover, theatre), maybe you miss a day of work, their little sister misses dance practice, then you reward them with some Shake Shack, and then never hear back on how any of the auditions went. Or you see on social media that her best friend booked the job. Or another stage mom is asking you why your daughter didn't get an audition for that TV show. Or conversely, you could be on a plane for a screen test the next day, then book a series regular on a new show, you relocate your family to another state, and they could be on TV for the next five years. Alternatively, you fly to LA, screen test, they do not book the job, then go back to school the next day like it never happened. But now you are down sick days, you missed your best friend's wedding, and it's good times all around. Just keeping it real, as this is what I see on a daily basis. It's a grind. And some parents have *five* kids in the business (bring on the wine).

If your kids work a Broadway schedule, then they already understand work ethic. If they don't, then here's the deal. When they are a young actor with an agent or manager, they are essentially a *freelance* worker. This means when they get an audition, they need to drop everything else to prepare for it, as that is the contract you both signed. It means they should treat every audition as an opportunity to grow, learn, put their best foot forward, compete, and then they could end up on a commercial or TV show. It's very exciting and will teach them so many skills that will help them in life. Now if you say no to that agent or manager because there's a talent show at school or you have to bring your other kid to the dentist, you are now saying that these opportunities are not a priority and they will stop sending you auditions. Especially if it becomes a pattern. Remember, agents and managers only make money when your kids book, so if they are working tirelessly to get you in the room (a big feat), and they finally do, and you tell them you can't make it, it never goes well and a tough conversation soon follows.

I have worked with a lot of kids and teens as an on-set coach after they have booked jobs on major television shows, and it's the first time they have ever stepped on set. The director doesn't have the time to make sure they are ready and that their energy is up. Suddenly your kid is playing a major recurring role on a big TV show, with some big stars. They are now working. With a real job comes real responsibility. And if the show is a hit, they are suddenly working with a lawyer, publicist, agent, manager, business manager, Comic-Con manager, and they are being pulled in different directions, all the while banking their school hours with a tutor on set. It's an adult world, and it's a lot of responsibility. That means when the director calls, "Cut," they have to keep working. They have to make up their schoolwork on set, in 20-minute increments. It's stressful and exhausting. Sometimes the kid goes on break, only to have everyone come by with notes—the director, the acting coach (me), the dialect coach, hair and makeup, all the while the tutor is demanding they "bank school hours."

During a busy pilot season, you might be tearing your hair out running around the city with last-minute auditions, scripts constantly changing, carrying different colored shirts around with you, getting into arguments, doing tons of self-tapes, getting stuck in traffic (while your kid is Facetiming with their acting coach), missing deadlines, all the while wondering is it worth it? The answer is: it depends. Are they enjoying it? Do they like memorizing sides at the last minute and walking into different rooms and acting in front of strangers? Do they care if they get the job or not? Are they stressed and putting too much pressure on themselves? Are you putting too much pressure on them? Are they driving the boat, or are you? And do me a favor: don't get caught up in the other b.s. in the waiting room with the other parents. Everyone loves to talk about what their kids are working on, and it can make other kids and parents feel insecure. Put on some headphones, listen to a meditation podcast (I like *Meditation Oasis*) and ignore it. It's all fake.

Most importantly, we need to take off as much of the pressure as possible. We don't ever need to say, "this is a big audition" to them, as it adds unnecessary nerves and anxiety, and makes them stiff in the room. It's just another normal day, and you will go get ice cream after because they worked hard and you worked hard. The second they feel pressure, they turn into robots (I see this all the time), and they need to be relaxed, free, and be their authentic selves every time they walk into the room.

Work hours on set

Here is how TV working hours are broken down:

If you are less than 6 years old, you are only allowed to work 6 hours total (between being on set and schoolwork).

If you are less than 9 years old, you are only allowed to work 8 hours total (between being on set and schoolwork).

If you are between 9 and 16, you are allowed 9 total hours on set total (between being on set and schoolwork).

If you are between 16 and 18, you are allowed 10 hours on set in total (between being on set and schoolwork).

Passing on auditions

It's better to send in two *killer* self-tapes than five *mediocre* ones. If it's a busy season, and your son or daughter is getting tons of auditions, and can barely keep up, it's more than okay to call your manager or agent and say, "I need to pass on some of these. Which do you think is the most important?" It's better this way, trust me. Your reps will appreciate this, as often times they won't even bother sending in a tape that isn't great (it's a reflection on them, after all).

I find the most successful kids and teens I work with are the ones that have a life outside of acting. They go to soccer camp, they go on vacations (and book out with their agents), they don't obsess about the acting world, and they aren't sure if they are going to do this after high school. They are being kids, they are being themselves, and that is the most attractive quality to a casting director. Casting directors, producers, and directors are always looking for "real kids". Not "actors". That's why they ask for personality slates at the beginning of some auditions (the ones casting asks them questions). They want to see what your son or daughter is like when they are being themselves, and not *acting*.

The goal of any audition is to make the scene feel new, unrehearsed, and spontaneous. The last thing they want to see is a kid who is stressed out, overcoached, and tired. If they are getting to this point, it's beyond okay to call your agent and tell them you want to take a break for a few months. The agent will always be there, and auditions will always be there.

If you have an agent and aren't getting many auditions at all, then it's time to sit down with your reps and ask them, "What can we do to increase our chances of getting more appointments? Do we need new headshots? New footage? Should they be in a class?" I find that so many parents and kids don't have this conversation and haven't seen their agent or manager in over a year (and their son or daughter has grown 12 inches). How can they pitch you if they don't even know what you look like anymore? Stop by the office, say hello, and don't feel weird about it. They work for you, and if you have a contract (or even if you don't), you are entitled to some face to face time.

The dead zone

There is this weird period for kids between the ages of 13 and 17 called the "Dead Zone." Creepy, right? It means it's a tough age to book jobs. Once a kid becomes a teenager, it usually makes more sense for a union film or television show to hire a kid who is at least 18 to play younger. It's cheaper and they can work more hours. If you hire a teenager who is a union actor, you can only use them for a small number of hours, and production has to pay for a tutor as well if it's during school time. It can get expensive. This means there are fewer auditions during this time period, which is a great time for kids to take classes, pick up some hobbies, get involved in some plays or musicals, build confidence, and get ready for when they turn 18. This doesn't mean the jobs don't exist, it just means it's a highly saturated category and not a great time to be looking for a new agent.

If you don't have an agent or manager

You are young, and now is the time to build credits. Get comfortable on the stage or in front of the camera, before you ask to be thrown into the big leagues. Do some student films, take some classes, but be careful you don't get "overcoached" (which turns a natural young kid into a "performer," making them less hirable in the on-camera world). When you feel like you are ready, and want to pursue representation, look up the websites of youth talent agencies in the area you live in. A lot of them have direct submission links, where they ask for an email with a picture, resume, and recent footage if you have it. If they are interested, they will call. Sometimes these agents already have 10 kids that look just like you. Sometimes you are exactly what they are looking for. Who knows? Remember, you might suddenly be going on five commercial auditions a week, so be sure you are ready for the sacrifice that comes with this.

Chapter 16: Reality Check
Hard Core Truths About Being a Professional Actor

1. You will have 15 pages to memorize for an audition, and when you show up, they will tell you that you are only reading half of the last scene.

2. You will prepare 20 pages of sides and show up only to find out your manager forgot to give you the "revised pages."

3. They will ask you to read for 4 other roles "while you are waiting."

4. Casting directors will say, "Nice to meet you," even though you have met them 43 times.

5. On your way to an audition, they will cancel your appointment because the role has been cast.

6. On your way to an audition, they will cancel an audition because they changed the age, gender, and/or ethnicity.

7. Your friends will go on more auditions than you. Always.

8. Your agent will tell you they aren't giving feedback during pilot season.

9. Your manager will tell you, "it's going to get really crazy," and it won't.

10. You will think about firing your agent and manager on a daily basis.

11. You will book a pilot, only to be fired after the table read.

12. You will book a pilot, the show will get picked up, and you will be recast.

13. Your parents will ask what a pilot is and wonder when they are going to see you on TV.

14. You will be asked to screen test, get a quote, sign a contract for the next seven years of your life, see how much money you will make, including backend points and salary bumps, fly out to LA to read for the network test, not get the job, and then be going on a Taco Bell audition the next day.

15. You will be sitting in a waiting room before an audition, and you will hear the assistant talking to an agent on the phone and making an offer to someone else for the role.

16. You will be told that every casting director "LOVES you."

17. You will go on tape, and the next day have a Skype callback with the creative team. And that will happen five more times before you find out they went with someone younger.

18. You will go on tape 150 times and never hear anything.

19. You will be in waiting rooms with 50 people that look just like you, dress like you, talk like you, and have better agents than you.

20. Your agent will never return your calls.

21. Your manager will return your calls a week later.

22. Your mom will always return your calls.

23. You will probably get fired from your survival job because your auditions are getting in the way.

24. You will be asked not to worry about the accent, and then be asked to "just go for it" in the audition.

25. You will read a breakdown and say, "that's me!" And so will everyone else.

26. You will go through 1,046 emotions on a daily basis.

27. You will hear, "They are going another way" 1,046 times.

28. You will consider doing extra work.

29. You will constantly bitch about "the state of current TV" to your friends.

30. You will consider going Fi-Core.

31. "Too tall, too thin, too gay, not gay enough, too macho, not street smart, too 'cable,' no charisma, a bit thick, not feeling it, not a fan, big fan, a bit shiny." All feedback. All real.

32. You will break up with your significant other because they "don't understand your career".

33. You will self-tape while sitting on the toilet.

34. You will freelance with 10 agents and audition once a year.

35. You will be sitting in a makeup chair on set, and the makeup person will ask you, "what's wrong with your skin?" right before your closeup.

36. You will act across from a piece of tape on set.

37. Once a year someone you know will get food poisoning from Craft Service on set.

38. You will consider paying for social media followers to make yourself more hirable.

39. You will ask your friends to click on your IMDB page to raise your Star Meter ranking.

40. Everyone you know will be asking you to donate to their short film.

41. You will use these at least once: #blessed #actorslife.

Chapter 17:   Interview with a TV/Film Casting Director
Stephanie Holbrook

I recently sat down with Stephanie to ask the questions that actors are dying to know the answers to. Here is her really long bio. Yeah, she's that good.

Stephanie Holbrook is a Casting Director with extensive credits in both film and TV. Currently, Stephanie is the Casting Director for *The Sinner* on the USA Network, now in its third season, and is co-casting *Servant* for M. Night Shyamalan, part of the first slate of series produced for Apple TV's new streaming platform. A member of the Casting Society of America, Stephanie is a multiple-nominee and multiple-winner for Excellence in Casting. She has numerous film credits that have premiered at the Sundance Film Festival, most recently *The Wolf Hour* and *Abe* in 2019. Stephanie also recently cast *Human Capital,* which premiered at the Toronto International Film Festival this year. Prior, Stephanie cast *The Kindergarten Teacher* and *Madeline's Madeline,* both Sundance 2018 and for which Stephanie earned Artios Awards, given to her by her peers. Past film credits include *My Friend Dahmer* (Tribeca 2017), *Equity*, *Christine*, and *The Eyes of My Mother* (all Sundance 2016), *Life Of Crime, The Lifeguard, Applesauce, Ghost Team, Ratter, Ava's Possessions, The Abandoned, Jane Wants a Boyfriend, The Happening* for M Night Shyamalan, *Book of Love, Ordinary World, Three Generations, Catfight (*Toronto International Film Festival), *Landline* and *Thoroughbreds* (both Sundance films). Earlier in her career, Stephanie was on the casting team for *Glass, Isle of Dogs, The Life Aquatic with Steve Zissou, We Own The Night, The Squid and The Whale, Margot at the Wedding, Margaret, Failure to Launch, The Village* and *Lady In the Water*, among others.

Me: How has your casting business changed since Covid?

There was a period of time where everything stood still. But then, indie films shooting in 2021 continued to cast. I also cast two films during "quarantine" that shot in Canada over the summer with strict Covid protocols.

Me: What advice can you give to actors during this transitory period?
Keep working and collaborating as much as possible, be it via zoom or socially distanced scene study. Participate in online projects and keep looking for those auditions because things are picking up.

Me: How has Zoom changed things for you?

I have learned to let go of the organic experience of being in the room with actors. It has provided more time for creative thinking as time spent commuting has gone away. It's made the audition experience less an energy exchange and stripped it down to the performance almost solely. It's made it possible to do chemistry reads and callbacks in a time where we simply can't be in the room with each other.

Me: What are your thoughts on actors and auditioning?

If you're talking about what can go wrong, sometimes I feel like actors overthink, and try to ask too many questions, and it's just so simple. All you have to do is take what's on the page in front of you, find the truth for you in the scene (based on what's on the page). If you have no questions answered, no idea what happened before, or where it's going next, you create that for yourself. I think what I see a lot is actors putting a lot of pressure on themselves trying to determine what the answers are, when really we want to see what your choices are, what you do, what your energy is, how you bring that page to life in an authentic way.

Me: Is it as simple as a "vibe?"

Yes, but sometimes you look at the page, and try to figure out the "vibe," and it's actually something different. And sometimes the scene isn't something from the actual project. So we want you to bring something uniquely you. There are constant rewrites. Your job is just to look at what's there and try to bring your own truth to the material. And then we find ourselves saying "yes, that's it!"

Me: So, someone's gonna roll in, not be off book, and totally have the right vibe, and they will make it work.

Exactly. Because the idea is to find the actor who feels most right for a role innately, and that may not be the person described on the page.

Me: So, actors need to relax and not obsess?

Yes. I'm in a situation right now on a project, where four actors are up for a young version of an older actor. One of the actors knocked it out of the park, two of them weren't right acting or looks-wise. The one who looks like the actor the most did not nail it. They did a Skype audition, he was a mess, got the audition time wrong, but they gave him another chance, because physically he is so right for it, and in this case, that was a priority. We are giving this guy a break, even though he wasn't on his game on the first call.

Me: How much do headshots matter?

Not that much except they have to look like you. That's it.

Me: So, does it matter if someone spent $1500 on a headshot, that's going to show up on the breakdowns as a little jpeg?

Not to me.

Me: Will you bring in people for one line you have never met?

Yes, I do it all the time.

Me: Why?

Because, to be frank, I don't always know a lot of those people. The ones willing to do one line who are just getting started.

Me: Why would you fill your time slots and bring in people you don't know with small agencies for one line when you have people you know from bigger agencies who you trust?

Because they look right and might be awesome. We need bodies.

Me: How many an episode?

Sometimes 40.

Me: How many people will you see for a one-line role?

30. Sometimes 40. Depends how much time we have to cast it.

Me: What's the worst thing an actor can do with a one-line role in an audition?

Make a meal out of it. Which happens all the time.

Me: Just do it.

Yes.

Me: Have you seen actors butcher that audition?

Of the 40 people I could bring in, half of them could butcher it. But the other half could go on the link!

Me: Would you bring them in again?

I think I would take a look at a resume. I understand how hard it is to come in and do one line and put all that pressure on yourself. I've seen people try to shove four different emotions into a ten-word line. I'm very honest with them. I say: "Pick one."

Me: Do you look at resumes for the people you bring in for one line?

Yes. Because if 400 actors have been submitted, I need to whittle it down to 30.

Me: Do you ever look at demo footage?

Absolutely. I will look at 10 seconds.

Me: Does it matter what the footage is from?

If this person is gonna be in a scene with Bill Pullman, or an actor of note, I will care more. There are enough people who are submitted for one line who actually have professional scenes. However, if I'm looking for a very small role, and haven't found it—anything that brings the actor to life, whether it's footage from a class, anything can help give me an idea of that actor's energy.

Me: Do you recommend people spend $2000 to create a fake scene to get in front of you for one line?

No. I'm telling you, if you are right for it, and I'm having trouble casting it, and you are giving me a video chat of yourself, I'm fine.

Me: Do you think actors should pay to meet casting directors?

That's a tough one. I have taught those classes. I have met a lot of actors that way and have brought a lot of actors in that way. I don't think everyone does. I think it's...helpful to do those classes, and it's important to meet busy casting directors, because you know they are going to have a good perspective and are working on a show and seeing lots of people. I would be very careful about it, however.

Me: Why would you bring in someone from a casting workshop if you get all these submissions from reputable agencies? Why take the chance?

Because I'm in a room with them, I get to work with them. At least in my classes, I interact with them. I do two-week classes, so I can actually see them do several scenes, with different tones, and actually see them work, instead of them just coming in one time with whatever they have chosen.

Me: What's the one piece of advice you want to give any actor who wants to be on TV?

Flex your muscles, work as much as you can. Whether it's in a black box theatre in New York City, or anywhere. The more you work on your craft, the better it's going to be when you get in that room for a one-line role.

Me: What are the reasons your producers turn down an actor?

They may say, "They're trying too hard," "I don't see them in this world," "Their hair is too short and we don't have time to let them grow it out, and we don't have money to wig them," "They acted with their eyebrows." I've heard it all.

Me: Do you get upset when someone you love doesn't book it?

Yes. I could bring in an indie darling, who I think is really gonna hit, and they aren't interested.

Nowadays, there's like 10 people who have to weigh in on who is getting cast. You are talking about a studio and a network working together on a television show, and you are trying to appease the upper echelon of Execs as well as the Casting Execs, as well as the creative team (Director, Showrunner).

It's my job to fight for the actors I think would be great but sometimes we Casting Directors are outruled.

Me: How has everything changed with casting in the last ten years?

Actors are not getting paid as much, everyone's trying to churn out as much content as possible for as little money as possible, so everyone's getting a smaller paycheck. There are also now a zillion cooks in the kitchen making decisions.

Me: So, essence is most important?

Yes. So much of my job is finding an actor's natural essence that brings the character to life in an authentic way.

Me: What if an actor is difficult in the room but right for the job?

Even if they are totally high maintenance, we will still submit their tape, because there is something special. You can't always take the risk in TV of sending someone to set who's a little quirky because of time constraints and the parameters of TV shoots...but for film I would. And I will tell the team "This person was high maintenance in the room, I recommend a meeting prior."

Me: How much does outfit color matter?

Not much, it just shouldn't be distracting. Watch out for busy accessories as well.

Me: Do you look at self-tapes?

Always. You have to nowadays. Everyone is everywhere.

Me: What's a good self-tape?

Simple, not overproduced, not distracting in any way. People do not need to set up a whole movie. It should mirror the experience in the room. It doesn't need to be high tech.

Me: You can see talent through anything.

Yes. And if need be, I can say, "re-tape with these three notes, better lighting, and better audio." As long as I can see you and hear you, and the reader isn't distracting.

Me: What's the most amount of submissions you have ever gotten for a role?

Maybe 4800? High profile director.

Me: How many will you bring in?

For a substantial role could be like 400. In-person or self-tape.

Me: Any last piece of advice for actors who are breaking in?

Keep working.

Chapter 18: Interview with a Theatrical Talent Agent
Robert Attermann from A3 Artists Agency

I recently sat down with my friend Robert Attermann (who used to represent me at Abrams Artists Agency, and yeah, he picked up my calls) to get some candid answers to some important questions. Robert has been an agent for over 30 years. He purchased the company in 2018, rebranding the company as one complete office between NY and LA (now called A3 Artists Agency). They have over 80 agents now, representing adult and youth talent, TV and film lit, theatrical lit, unscripted, adult and youth commercial and voice over, podcast studios on both coasts, digital, influencers, books, and a colony devoted to developing artists' projects. He knows his shit.

Me: How has your casting business changed since Covid?

It has slowed down. Zoom auditions, self-tapes and reels are much more prevalent now rather than in person auditions.

Me: What advice can you give to actors during this transitory period?

Stay calm, take audition classes online if you can, watch TV and movies, see what's out there. Read online industry news and see what's happening in the business, keep in shape mentally and physically.

Me: How has Zoom changed things for you?

It's a lifeline to keeping in communication. It's a way to maintain meetings inter and intra office. It's a way to see everyone rather than just speaking with them on a phone.

Me: How has TV/Film/Theatre changed in the last ten years?

It has changed a lot. There are more TV shows on many different platforms. Movies have smaller budgets and there are less big budgeted films. Theatre is always busy. The audiences in all three mediums have become more sophisticated and demand better quality programming, films and theatre. There is so much more content to place actors, directors and production people into. More jobs.

Me: Do you think it's harder for a newer actor to book a pilot?

Since there is more content looking for actors, no it's not harder. More name actors are looking to get into TV so the competition for lead roles is there. There are many supporting characters for newer actors to book.

During pilot season, they are looking for new people. It's like an open call. I think anyone can book a pilot, whether you just started or have lots of experience.

Me: Do you think actors should do co-star roles?

Just a couple in the beginning, get your feet wet, use it as a learning experience. Get paid to learn. Do just a few, no more.

Me: What do you expect from your clients?

Be prepared. Show up on time. Be the best you can be at the audition. Don't be difficult to work with. This is your job, take it seriously and work at 200%.

Me: What do you say to an actor who has been auditioning for a while and not booking?

They should take an audition class to make sure they are auditioning properly. The more frustrated an actor gets, the worse they get at auditioning. They get uptight. As long as you are getting callbacks, you are eventually gonna book something.

Me: What makes you drop a client?

It's very hard for me to drop a client, because you never know. If someone goes on many auditions, and the feedback isn't good. Or they aren't nice. They get in their own way.

Me: What do you think about actors calling you up and asking to submit them for a role?

I say: have you read the script? Do you know anything about it? The breakdown doesn't mean anything. It always changes. The breakdown could come out today, change this afternoon. I know they are being active to make sure they are submitted on every appropriate project, so I welcome the ask.

Me: What drives you nuts?

When an actor sees a movie or TV show, calls me up the next day, and says, "Why wasn't I submitted for that?" And it's a role that Tom Hanks is playing.

Me: Do you think actors should pay to meet agents and casting directors?

That's an interesting question. I think it can be a good opportunity to really learn, as long as they aren't charging a ridiculous amount of money.

Me: Do you think actors should be creating their own work on the side while waiting for auditions?

100%. Keep busy and keep networking and clear your head.

Me: What else should they be doing?

Make money to pay their rent. Take acting classes. Read the trades, know the business, watch TV, go to movies, go to the theatre. See what's out there.

Me: Do actors need to be in LA?

Nope. Actors are cast all over the world. Actors can tape, Skype, and don't need to always be in the room.

Me: What makes a good self-tape?

Decent lighting, be off book, brief and always to the point.

Me: Should actors ask for feedback?

Unless they were horrible, we won't get much besides, "They were great, just not the right fit." Unless someone is down to the second callback, then we'll find out what happened.

Me: How important are headshots?

People look at them. Make sure the headshot looks like you.

Me: What advice do you have for actors breaking into the business?

The most important thing is to have patience, be diligent, don't be difficult, read as much as you can about the business, take some classes (especially audition classes), and just be aware of everything that's going on in the business.

Me: What kind of footage should an actor have? Should they spend tons of money to produce a scene?

No. They are looking at 10 seconds of it. Put recent work. Make sure you are in the scene.

Me: What's the one thing you want all actors to know?

Don't expect to become a star overnight. We have actors that have been around for twenty years and are suddenly now making it big. Be patient. If you aren't making progress, you should reevaluate what you are doing. But if you are making progress, getting callbacks, getting close, then keep going.

Chapter 19: Interview with a Youth Talent Manager
Peggy Becker from Parkside Talent

Peggy and I share a lot of clients, and I think she is one of the most honest, loyal, hardworking managers out there. Peggy Becker (Parkside Talent) has been a talent manager/owner for over a decade. Parkside has placed talent in projects from Broadway, film, TV series, commercials, voiceovers and print. The company has expanded into adults as well. Now listen up and take notes.

Me: How has your business changed since Covid?

The business has changed in our industry a lot. People are working from home. Castings are done online. Studios are now being built in talent's homes. Everything now has been virtual.

Me: What advice can you give to actors during this transitory period?

Create your dream project, jump on that zoom class, learn how to use all of the new technology, read the trade magazines (online).

Me: How has Zoom changed things for you?

It has helped me to learn a lot about technology. It has led me to have conversations with people about possibilities that before weren't necessarily possible. It made me realize that I can accomplish more now than before.

Me: What's the best part about being a manager?

Best part about being a manager is the honor of making a difference for that person. A new actor who has no idea, everything's all raw, and they come to you for help and for guidance. I love that talent come to me for an opportunity to transform their lives. They are looking for someone they can actually trust, knowing that you are going to support them and guide them to a career.

Me: What does a manager do?

Day to day we organize schedules, submit talent to casting, manage schedules, put out "fires." A manager's job I feel is to make everything right for the client. We educate, we invent their careers, we take their strong points and we align people with them to help support their goals, we vet photographers, acting coaches, publicists, stylists, grooming, car services etc. We try to keep the industry as safe as possible in knowing the people we are getting involved in. We do a lot of research.

Me: How has the business changed over the years?

The business has changed dramatically. It is almost entirely internet based now. A manager is the source of everything. The manager creates a team that will best negotiate for the client.

Me: You can't actually negotiate?

Managers can't negotiate. An agent has to do that.

Me: What if the actor doesn't have an agent?

We get them one.

Me: Just for that one job?

No, we make sure the client will be taken care of for future projects. Most of our clients have agents though.

Me: Even if it's a small job?

Yes.

Me: Do all managers do that?

There are managers who do their own negotiating.

Me: Even though it's unprofessional?

Yes.

Me: So, it's an unspoken thing?

Yes.

Me: Do you think there will be a day where all managers will be allowed to negotiate?

Yes. Fast approaching. The whole industry is changing.

Me: Okay. So, what if I have a kid who wants to break into the business. What would you tell them?

I would want to meet them. I would want to see if the child really wants to be in this business or is it mom/dad pushing them into it. I would then tell them that it is a very hard business. There is A LOT of rejection. If they still want to do this out of the love to perform and they have talent, then I will help them.

Me: What's the difference between a kid who is in a local play at school, versus someone who is ready to be auditioning for TV?

That's interesting. If I go to the school play, the children who are right for this industry glow like lightbulbs. You have to train yourself as a representative to see who glows like lightbulbs. The children in the school play normally love to perform. A child ready to audition, has been trained in acting.

Me: I never did anything professional until I was 23. What is the thing you see when watching a kid?

There's a charisma/it factor (as some call it). There is something in a way that a child acts in a natural environment, where they can take a script and translate it into real life, and you believe them.

Me: What happens when a kid you work with suddenly books a really big job? What changes?

Everything changes. We have to prepare them for those changes. Managers at that point have to create a whole new life for them.

Me: What's the most a kid can make as a network level series regular for the first year?

That would depend on the network, project, and the child's resume.

Me: How has social media affected the business? Do you tell your clients to be on social media?

Social media can be a great tool if used properly. It has become a necessity in our business. We monitor our client's social media. We have found that social media can be our best friend and our worst enemy.

Me: Do you think there will come a time where kids will need to post the number of followers they have on their resume?

I hope not.

Me: Here are some rapid-fire questions. Number one pet peeve of your clients?

"Why wasn't my child submitted?"

Me: What's your number one pet peeve of actors submitting to you?

If they submit a resume to me with another manager listed on it. We don't play like that.

Me: Why do you drop clients?

I drop clients if the parents or the clients are unprofessional.

Me: What's that mean?

I mean if the client poses risks to other talent or if the client did something that was iniquitous, that is really the only reason I would drop a client.

Me: Yikes. What's a harsh reality of the business?

It is a really tough business to make it in. There is more rejection in our business that actors have to face every day that isn't prevalent in other businesses.

Me: Do you think actors should do pay-to-meet workshops?

No! Not at all.

Me: What makes a great self-tape?

A Matt Newton tape. Haha. It has to have good lighting, be clear, the actor needs to be off book, presenting his or her best self. You have to have done your research into the character, have a better understanding of how you are going to play the character, and go to a coach to work out the scenes. The tape itself has to look professional.

Me: Cell phone tapes?

I would prefer not.

Me: Do you always recommend actors get coached?

Yes. Actors get caught in a pattern, and develop a habitual way of acting, and it only gets them so far. They have to be present, and when they work with an acting coach, the coach breaks you out of the way of always doing it and drives you to the depths of where you can't get to by yourself.

Me: True. Anything else you want to say?

There is a lot to say.

Me: Don't be an asshole?

NO, please don't be an asshole to us. We are your team. We can only pitch a package of you if the package is complete. If your headshots are horrible, your resume is bare, and you are sitting on your butt waiting for us to do something, that doesn't work.

Me: What do you expect clients to be doing while waiting for auditions?

For kids...I want them to be doing summer camp, I want them to be doing soccer, I want them to do baseball, I don't want their whole youth to be musical theatre camp, signing, acting, dancing. I don't want that. I don't want kids to go to musical theatre school for college. There is a whole other world outside of that. Go explore. When they see the competition and get so mono-focused on how it should be, it's just so detrimental to the actor. They pigeonhole themselves. For adults...get involved in that reading, that play, meet people. Do student films, work on that production with your friends. Stop asking for the world to give it to you. Go create something.

Chapter 20: Conversation with an Editor
Howard Leder from NBC's "This is Us"

Howard Leder is the editor of the hit show "This is Us". He has also worked on "The Newsroom," "Big Love" (HBO), "American Gods" (Starz), "The Killing" (AMC) as well as the pilot for "Pitch" (Fox). He's also an actor, and super funny.

Me: When you're a day player or a guest star on a long-running show like "This is Us," there are nerves that can creep in when you are on set. What advice would you give to an actor in that situation?

Fall back on your training. As long as it feels like it's coming from you, it's grounded, it's deliberate, it's clear, you know, anything is within bounds for me. I love watching variation, seeing all the subtle choices people make. That said, I've seen some day players come in and they just make these crazy choices, and I'm like "I don't know what to do with this..."

Me: Do you see a lot of nerves in footage?

Yeah, it typically looks like "I don't know my lines" - that's the big thing. I've seen guest stars come in for "This is Us" and think "OMG, those five people are in front of me," and the actor's preparation just goes.

Me: How do you still edit the performance to make it work in that case?

The thing about editing that's so wonderful is that there is no performance that can't be improved or fixed through editing. That's what we're there for. One of the telling words we use in the cutting room is "protect". Nobody ever says "Can you make that person better?" It's "Can you protect that performance?" So, I go in and really look for the places where they're on, they're present, they're committed, they're completely in the scene, where they're listening. Sometimes those moments are only 2 seconds long. I don't need 10 seconds of a close up - unless you're Milo Ventimiglia in which case I'll take 20 seconds of a close up! But you know, that's really all I need. If I can find those moments, I can begin to shape a performance for you that is completely believable and also very moving.

Me: Do you think a lot of actors, maybe newer actors, do too much in a closeup?

I have a friend who's an editor, who used to be my assistant editor, who's now working principally in features. His way of saying this is "Lean into the subtle." The thing to always remember is that the camera, in a closeup in particular, can see you think, and that sounds like magical hoo-haa, but it's absolutely true. It can see the thoughts in your head, but we can also feel you breathe, these microphones are so close to you… A lot of my time in the editing room is spent shaping the breath of an actor. There are some actors who are super heavy breathers, and you'll get notes like "Can you take all that breathing out?" But also, when you're acting and you have a thought and you breathe in, that's where the line begins, you know? So those breaths can become important to the editor as much as the line, often more important than the line. There are certain scenes I've done where we end up cutting 50-60% of the dialogue, and just going with, you know, a sigh, an inhalation, a look of surprise, it says as much as a whole paragraph of dialogue and you're like "I don't need that, that actor is just talking right now." But that moment of sighing tells me as much as anything.

Me: How important are nonverbal moments in a scene?

One of the ways I taught myself to edit, and I think this is something actors would benefit from too, is I watch movies and television shows with the sound off. That is like one of the greatest film schools I've ever been to. If you rely on the words to tell the story, okay. But really, it's the face. It's the feelings you're having and the thoughts you're having and the reactions you're having. That's where the movie or the television show lives. That's what we pay for when we watch movie stars - paying to watch somebody feel something in front of us. If you turn the sound off you unhook yourself from the dialogue - you're gonna be suddenly in touch with exactly what the actor is doing and know they picked that shot because of that. I'd say a great exercise is to pick a couple of your favorite actors and watch tv episodes or movies with the sound off and see how much information you get about that character, what you learn. You'll be amazed.

Me: What about continuity? Do actors need to pay attention to it?

Yes and no. They should worry about it... The thing to always remember is that 95% of the audience, there are the people who don't work in film and TV, and aren't trained to look at the complete frame (because people who work in TV are watching the WHOLE thing) - most of our focus is on the eyes and a little bit on the lips. If your hands are doing something funny, most of the time we're not gonna notice. It's when it gets closer to your face that it starts becoming an issue. This is why food scenes are always tricky. I jokingly say: "If God had wanted perfect continuity, he wouldn't have given actors hands." I think if you're doing something that's dealing with your face, or your hair, then it can become a real problem. If someone touches your face, and doesn't do it on the other side, now I have a problem. Wearing glasses in a take and not wearing glasses in a take - now I've got a huge problem. But take the buttoned or unbuttoned shirt, I would probably be like, some people are going to notice that, some aren't - let them point it out on IMDb, bravo for them. But if the producers notice, then you do have to start fixing it. And there's a million ways to fix that. The hardest thing to deal with in terms of continuity is if you change a place where you say the line. If you come through the door and say a line in one take, and on the next take you come through the door and walk into the middle of the room and say the line - I can't solve that, you know? That's where it really gets tricky. But I WILL solve it!

Me: How much should actors worry about their frame?

The actors on our show have this kind of uncanny sense of the camera - I think that's just an experience thing. I mean Milo clearly knows where the camera is at all times and exactly what lens he's on and how much clearance there is and stuff like that. I think that's something that the DP,

100

as much as the editor, is looking out for you. She or he should be saying, "Oh, you're falling out of frame here."

Me: What was it like in the editing room for "Newsroom?" How much do actors have to worry about being word-perfect?

Well, the Sorkin actors are chosen for that ability. They're cast based on that sort of thing, you know? The other things to remember is that Aaron was an actor, he loves actors, he adores actors, the actors/characters are his best friends. They were told and I was told that they needed to be word perfect, and if they weren't word perfect, we were supposed to report that. But there was never anything like that, I mean I'm not going to walk in and say "Um, Jeff Daniels changed "the" to "a."

Me: I know actors who have been cut out of a TV show. How do you deal with having to cut down an actor's part?

The worst-case scenario is that you get cut out entirely. The big thing to remember is that 50-60% of the time it's not you. It's the script, it's the directing. A show like "This Is Us" in particular, we have to fit in a 42-minute time slot. Our rough cuts, our first assemblies, are 55-57 minutes long. Every performance in a show is getting squeezed - the stars are getting squeezed, everything that is not crucial, is gonna get cut to the bone. And very often, if you're a day player, or you're just in one scene, you're probably there to deliver some kind of information to which Mandy Moore is going to have a reaction. Her reaction is the most important part of the scene. If you're playing a doctor, let's say, and you've got 15 lines of exposition about what's wrong with your kid, those 15 lines are going to get cut to the minimum. Because what we're wanting to see is our character who we've been with for four years, how they're reacting to that. So, I would never blame myself first. There are so many other issues. You have to always be thinking in three, four dimensions - what is the actual story of the scene?

Me: How important is listening in a scene?

I worked on "Big Love" which is kind of a masterclass in listening. It a huge cast, there's rarely fewer than 3 people in a scene, there's often 5, sometimes there's 8-10. There was this one scene in particular - it was Jeanne Tripplehorn, the great Ellen Burstyn, and this third woman who's name I do not know. But, thank God she was there. Because she was listening like a house on fire. She wasn't just listening, she was having an attitude, she was having a reaction, she was having a relationship in every single moment...and she maybe only had 5 or 6 lines in the scene, but the whole scene was 4-5 minutes. But she was a HUGE part of the scene, because she was constantly giving you something, constantly. I don't think she would know how to sit there and not give you something. She was fully engaged. She's having this whole other scene! I think that listening is the key. When I watch dailies, I keep my left hand on the keyboard, and I have a certain little marker that I can leave on the footage (a locator). It's kind of an instinctive response, that when I see something I can use, where the actor is clearly listening, or they have a moment where their eyes flicker trying to understand, when they look confused - just a tiniest little moment - I will mark those as I go along. So when I go back and look at a 3 minute take, it's like: there's a reaction, there's a reaction, there's a reaction... So when the producer says "Hey, do you have any other reactions on this person?", I'm like "Yeah, I have all of these set and ready to go". That saves me a lot of time. If you blink, if your eye twitches, if your mouth curls up, you cock your head in a strange way - those are the things that very often visually convey your thinking. Just stay engaged. And if you make an editor's job easier, they'll favor you.

Me: A lot of actors worry about being "perfect" on set, and not changing what they did in the callback. What do you think about that?

One of the very frustrating things with guest stars and day players is if the performances from take to take are exactly the same. I call it "tape recorder acting" where every single one has the same inflections, same movements, same rhythms, and same, same, same. Because very often the

102

bind that puts you in is that the producers will be like "Do you have anything else?" and you'll be like "No, but I have five others of the exact same thing". So then you're looking for such minute variations. So I think within a certain tolerance, you want to be playing and I think that's one of the things that makes a successful star a star. It's that, you could use, with Milo Ventimiglia, any one of the seven takes. They're all great! But there's one maybe that sticks out - but then the producers will come in and say "Is there one where he's a shave more angry?" and you just hope, you're just always hoping that you have those materials.

Me: You have a lot of young actors on your show who come in and do scenes with the veterans. What advice do you have on how to handle themselves?

I think in some sense, and I'm going to base this on my own experience as an actor, is that: remember that you're working with other actors who all had to go through the same journey. Whether they did that when they were 10, or whether they did that when they were in their 20s, or did it in their late 40s... They've all had to kind of make the same discoveries and learn the same lessons. Lean on that community. Those are the people you can learn from, more than I think potentially the director or the writers or whoever, who are worried about all these sort of giant issues, like "How am I gonna get this show on TV?" But really it's that community of actors, I would think, really just leaning on that.

Chapter 21: Stories from the Trenches
Audition Horror Stories from Working Actors

Here are some fantastic stories from some working actors I know. They wanted to leave their last names out, as some of them are a bit embarrassing.

To Die For

I auditioned for "To Die For" & had to simulate getting a blow job from Nicole Kidman while being convinced to kill her husband Matt Dillon. Joaquin Phoenix got the part!
-Jack, actor

Do the "Pony"

When I arrived in NYC I desperately wanted to do Broadway musicals. Since I had zero dance experience I firmly believed I fell into the category of "singers who move." "Hairspray" was having an open call for chorus members, and they were looking for quirky, off-beat actors. I put on my go-to outfit of camouflage pants, a boy scout shirt, and put my hair into double buns like Princess Leia. I even bought Capezio dance shoes for the occasion (even though when I got there everyone else was in sneakers). They did the dance portion of the audition first. I attempted to learn the combination, still convinced I could pull it off. They called us up in small groups to perform, and I not only got every step wrong, but proceeded to slam into and step on the feet of all the other actors auditioning with me, all while flailing my arms trying to do the "pony." I no longer consider myself a "singer who moves" unless I'm humming a tune while walking to Starbucks.
-Becki, actress

Christmas Lights

One of the memorable auditions I had was an appointment to read for a new TV series about mutants with super-powers. The character could generate electricity with his hands. The audition material was several pages long and the role I was reading for did most of the talking. I had one day's notice to prepare, and instead of fully reading the sides, I spent the day at a magic store. I was looking to find a specialty light bulb that concealed a battery and could be turned on in one's hand. This, I thought, was "my way in!" I would show up at the casting and as the audition started, I would light my hands up and be fully in character. I cringe as I recall walking into the audition with something literally "up my sleeve." I made my way in front of the camera and on "action," my brilliant idea wouldn't "turn on." I tried in vain to covertly fiddle with the switch but to no avail. I was red and sweating, not only because I was in a room full of people staring at me, but also because it was August and I was wearing a heavy leather jacket to conceal my stupid trick that wouldn't work. The casting director reminded me that I had the first line and I stood there, knees shaking, with my face buried in the page trying to make sense of a scene I had scantly read. The audition trudged on, and as the scene neared its end, I was determined to get the light bulb to turn on and so I held the pages lower to obscure the vision of the casting director and with one final fidget, the bulb turned on as if to illuminate the dreadful performance. "What do you have in your jacket?" she asked. "Is that...a...is that a light bulb? Why?" At this point I figured my handiwork had impressed them, so I smugly nodded my head as if to say, "You know it." They just looked baffled, offered a perfunctory, dismissive "thank you," and off I went thinking, "I nailed that!"
 -Chris, actor

Let's Give it a Rip!

My very first audition in NYC, fresh out of graduate school, was for a series regular role on a primetime network pilot. I received the material the day before the audition and immediately began to learn my lines. I spent hours poring over and over the seven pages of dialogue I was given.

I mapped out the location and made sure I would be in the waiting room 10-15 minutes before my audition was scheduled. On the day, everything worked to plan. I was ready. After all, I had spent 3 years in graduate school hammering on my craft. I had auditioned for plenty of plays and I naturally assumed that auditioning for television would be similar. I walked into the room, said hello to the casting director, her associate, and the camera operator. I made some small talk and then took my place on the marked "x" in front of the camera. After placing the mic in between buttons on my neatly pressed shirt, they asked me if I was ready, and with the forced bravado of a completely green actor, I said, "indeed, let's give it a rip!" What followed can only be described as an unmitigated disaster. Since I'd been drilling my lines so diligently, I figured I was completely off book. Therefore, my sides were confidently tucked in the back pocket of my jeans and not easily accessible. As soon as the scene started, I went blank and flubbed my first line. That initial misstep made me nervous, so my legs began to shake. No longer being grounded, I then began to pace back and forth. Not only was this unmotivated action a disservice to the scene, but the pacing caused me to walk in and out of frame. I immediately went into my head and began to watch myself, having what felt like an out of body experience in which I was watching my own train wreck without the ability to stop it or even slow it down. I finally turned away from the camera and, forgetting I was mic'd, muttered under my breath, "what the fuck am I doing?" After what seemed like an eternity, the scene was finished. I looked at the casting director, associate, and camera operator with cautious optimism, hoping it wasn't as bad to them as it felt to me. I was met with possibly the best/worst feedback I have received, even to this day, when the benevolent casting director paused and, searching for the right words, said, "Well, you.....uh.....well, you certainly did it." After a pause, I politely nodded and left the room. I didn't make it out of the building before my managers called me and invited me to stop by their office for a chat. Sure enough, I completely bombed. It took a while to get back into that office again. In the years that have passed since that humbling first step, I am constantly reminded of 3 things: 1) be off book, but always make sure your sides are in your hand. 2) stay grounded, stay in the scene, and don't worry about pleasing anyone but yourself. Do the work and be satisfied that you've adequately prepared ahead of time. 3)

don't crap on your own audition - especially when you're on a mic. If you do bomb an audition (everybody does) enjoy the process, smile, and know that you will have a story to share.
-Tom, actor

Cookie Monster

I bake Christmas cookies every year as my holiday gift to my agents and manager. It's a little unconventional from the usual baskets of cheese and chocolates they receive from most clients- but I'm Italian and love baking my grandmother's traditional Italian cookie recipes. So every year, with the help of my mom, we spend one or two whole days baking hundreds of cookies. We pack them into a bunch of tins and go into the city to give them to my agents. We usually bring extra tins to distribute to other New Yorkers who may be in need of some holiday cheer. One year I happened to have a big audition for a guest star role on a network TV show on the same day I planned to distribute my cookies. I have auditioned for the casting director many times before but had yet to book anything from their office. In the midst of my baking, I prepped my audition. I felt I knew the four pages of sides perfectly. Off book completely and with strong choices, I hauled my giant bag of cookie tins into NYC to visit my agents and rock the audition. After visiting with my agents, I had a few cookies tins left and headed to my audition. I was in the waiting room with about 20 other actors- it was a busy day in the office. While I prepped my lines some more and tried to expel all my nervous energy, an idea popped into my head. "I have extra cookies! I'll give the casting director a tin! What a nice gesture!" As I mentioned, I've been in for this casting director so many times, I didn't think it was weird to offer them cookies, I had extra and they're delicious! My name was called and with my sides and cookie tin in tow, I went into the room. Before starting I told the CD how I bake every year for my agents and had a few extra tins. I held the tin out to the CD, "Happy holidays! Would you like some cookies?" I asked. The CD responded with one single word, "No." I was so taken aback by the response and absolutely mortified. All of a sudden, thoughts came rushing to my mind, did the CD think I was being overzealous? Trying to get on their good side with cookies? What was I thinking!? What a terrible idea!

I tried to cover up my humiliation and put the cookies down. Almost in tears, I tried to collect myself quickly and did my scene. The lines I once knew perfectly and confidently came fumbling out of my mouth like word vomit. I had to pick up my script and practically read some of the lines directly from the page- something I never do. The CD asked me to do the second half of the scene again and "put a different spin on it." I quickly recalibrated and thought of a different choice, grateful for a second chance. Because of my nervousness and current lack of confidence, I also messed up my second take by having to read off the page yet again. I said thank you and picked up my cookies to go. As I was leaving, the CD said, "thank you for the cookie offer." I got into the elevator and broke down in tears not knowing what to think. Maybe the CD wasn't offended and I ruined my whole audition for nothing. Maybe I'd be black balled from the business because they thought I was trying to bribe them! I was convinced they would never call me in again. My manager called me the next day to ask me how it went and I told her my humiliating cookie story. She responded, "Well, you must not have done as bad as you thought because an offer just came in for you for the role." WHAT?! I was speechless. I booked the role! Even though my audition war story has a happy ending, I learned a lot from the experience. 1. Never offer a CD anything except maybe a thank you note after they cast you in something. 2. It's so, so easy to psych yourself out in the room so you can never be too prepared. 3. Don't be so hard on yourself if you think you bombed an audition. You never know what a casting director is thinking- even if you mess up the lines and think you just gave the worst audition ever. If you had strong choices from the start, they're probably always going to show though."
-Jordan, actress

Oompa Loompa

I got an appointment for a show and the CD's asked my agents if I could get a tan. YES, OF COURSE. I can't...I really can't. You don't get much fairer than me. But my agents suggested a spray tan. I went to the salon and stood in my underwear in front of the lady. She gave me a worried look and said, "she is going to do 1 coat of the lightest color they make." The next day, I was so orange I looked like an Oompa Loompa. I scrubbed

my skin till it was raw but couldn't get the orange blotches all the way off. Didn't get a callback for that either.
-Brittney, actress

Glam Queen

I was auditioning for a casting director that was great about calling me in. It was a really great role. It was more of a techy type character. Normally I would have not worn any makeup, but I decided you know what? If I was this person, I would fix myself up, even if my job wasn't glamorous. I went in, read for the role and she politely said she liked what I was bringing in, but would I kindly go to the bathroom and remove some of the eye makeup? Since that day I carry makeup wipes. Trying to take off makeup with hand soap and water is pretty rough.
-Myrna, actress

You Look Familiar

I was invited to a director's session. I felt I had the part and made some good strong choices. I picked just the right wardrobe. I felt good and ready. The day of the audition I got down to Chelsea about 30 minutes early (the audition was at Chelsea Piers) – I always leave myself a little wiggle room to be in the area so I can center myself and settle. I got an email from my manager which said, "Casting is running ahead and was wondering if you can get here early." I went straight to the session, instead of giving myself the time to settle. I walked in at 12:00 PM for a 12:20 audition. There were only 2 other people in the room. I figured I would be seen in the next 5 or 10 minutes. And then another 3 people came in and were all taken before me. I remember one of the people who had arrived after me had a drum and performed a whole number in the room. He was a former contestant on "American Idol" and spent time afterwards chatting up the other actors in the waiting room. All told, I waited for over an hour before I was invited into the room even though I had arrived early as requested. The whole time, I was trying to focus and ground myself. When I finally was brought into the room, all the work just

evaporated from my head. The take was spotty at best. Unrecognizable from what I had actually prepared. And that was it. In a flash, it was over. The director walked up to me at the end and said, 'Oh, I know you from (the show I recur on), I love you on that." It didn't make me feel any better, though.
-Chris, actor

The Stapler Dilemma

One time I went into an awesome pilot audition for ABC. It was my first pilot season and I had gotten four auditions in two days. I was doing my best to be off book for each audition no matter what. However, I was a bit confused about this particular one because the sides didn't make the most sense. Regardless, I hunkered down and prepped for it hoping that I could make sense of it immediately. When I got into the room, the CD asked me if I had any questions. I said, "Not really, but that story line is quite to the point!" The CD looked at me oddly and didn't respond to my comment. We started reading the audition and as soon as we turned the page to the third page - I was stopped by the CD who said, "You skipped a page." I was so confused because I had memorized this perfectly and we definitely did not skip a page. Turns out I had stapled my pages wrong and that's why nothing made sense. SO EMBARRASSING.
-Ajna, actress

Tootsie

It was 2009. I was still slinging drinks by night to scratch by enough dinero to keep the gas tank full as I ran around to countless auditions. It was mostly commercial auditions and it was a time where commercials made serious money. This fine day I was at my callback for AXE body spray and they were hiring at least 10 women for the spot, and many of us were already AVAIL- checked. Twelve of us signed in and stared at each other wondering who the hell was the one brave soul sitting there without a bathing suit cover-up on. Yes, it was required that we do this callback in our bikinis. I was the one self-consciously praying I would not get called in the room with the girl who was just sitting there

*smoking hot only in her bikini, aka Giselle. And then it happened,
"Alyshia and Giselle, you'll be on deck." After a few minutes, Giselle
sauntered into a room full of men. You know, the cameraman, casting
director, director and I swear 15 of his friends. Maybe they were the
client or maybe I was right. Just a bit coincidental there were so many
men there for a day of women running in their bikinis. The director gave
us a description of the spot. "You have been starving for months,
actually make it years, and you smell the most delicious piece of meat.
You are going to run over mountains and through forests, battling each
other to get to the piece of meat first. Okay, whenever you are ready.
Let's get to our bikinis." That was referenced only to me because Giselle
was just standing there glistening, with no sun even around, taking in
the directions. Smiling, knowing she has already booked the job. I
slowly walked across the room and pulled off my bathing suit cover-up. I
jiggled back to my spot next to Giselle, took a deep breath and waited
for the word "action." It was called and we started running in place.
"High knees, faster, shove each other a little bit" the director fervently
shouted at us. Then it happened. I farted. You heard that correctly, well
the whole room heard it correctly. BUT, don't you worry because I was
on my game. I had been taking a comedy class with Lesly Kahn and we
were starting every class with improv. This was a fast reaction to my
flagellation, my sharp improv skills showed up. I gasped and threw a
look to Giselle with the thought of "how could you fart Giselle." Then I
was gloating. Now I know I booked the job. And then it happened again.
Yup, I farted again and this time it was louder. I turned bright red. The
director yelled cut. Giselle sashayed out of the room. Their eyes did not
follow Giselle's perfect tushy, they stared and let out some giggles as I
shamelessly walked across the room to grab my cover-up. I slid down
the wall to hide the one part of my body that had betrayed me during
this audition. I whispered a "thank you" as I closed the door and heard
the room erupt with laughter. Needless to say, I did not book that job.
But you know what that audition did do for me...it made me realize I had
absolutely experienced the most hilarious thing that could ever happen
in an audition. That night at acting class all the actors sat around and
shared their highlights for the week. Now I was in class with some really
heavy hitters that were booking series regulars and big-time movies*

(aka the Armie Hammers and Abigail Spencers of the world) and when they got to me I shared that I had indeed farted in my audition not once, but actually twice. This filled the rest of the circle with some of the most hilarious and tragic auditions stories. It made me realize that this was the fun part of the career we never get to hear about. So let's start sharing the good, the bad and the ugly so we can continue to shine and not let one audition take us down. After farting in my audition I went on to star in the lead of a film (that year), do several TV shows and watch the AXE commercial play at the Superbowl. You win some, you lose some. Ha!
-Alyshia, actress

Who Wrote This Shit?

I learned very early on to keep my opinions to myself and to shut my mouth in auditions. Especially for musicals. It is not our job to judge the work, it is our job to do the work. One of my very first auditions was for a Broadway show. I was asked to learn new music written by some British composer I had never heard of. I was completely under prepared (learned that lesson too) and was not a fan of the music which, again, is not part of my job. Nevertheless, I went in and walked over to the piano before I sang. The accompanist apologized to me in advance and said, "I'm sorry about these few measures of music. I know they are difficult and weird. They are a work in progress." Thinking he was on my side and perhaps not a fan as well, I said, "oh my God, I am so relieved. It sucks, right? Ugh, just plunk it out as I go. I mean, honestly? Who wrote this shit?" He then replied, "I did. I wrote this shit." I did not get that job. That composer is very famous. I have never worked for him.
-Lesli, actress

In Closing: #pleasedontsuck
The Business of You

You have to treat your acting career as your business. You are the business owner, the entrepreneur, the breadwinner, the boss, the employee, and the unpaid intern. You have to work your ass off and do whatever is necessary to drop everything on a moment's notice and show up for that one audition. It could be the one. No more excuses. Nobody owes you anything, and there's far too many people out there who will work harder than you. Don't let that happen.

Figure out your finances, find a way to have flexibility and be diligent with your time. I am a firm believer in setting aside time each day to knock out your goals. Give yourself a half hour every morning, and use that time to submit, update, write, send emails, network, prep for auditions, whatever you need. Wake up every day and focus on one thing you can do to make yourself better. That doesn't mean sitting around doing monologues in your living room. That means taking care of the *business of you*. Go to the gym, get a haircut, turn off the *Love Island* marathon, practice your memorization, learn a new skill, pick up a hobby, meditate, learn to cook, stop obsessing, read a non-acting book, set some goals, and stop making excuses. Take the reins and be the best business owner you can be. Keeping yourself busy, happy, and inspired makes you a better actor and makes auditioning less *precious*.

An entrepreneur builds a business from the ground up, makes important decisions, course corrects along the way, and creates a path for the business to grow. You need to treat your career the same way. Feeling stuck in class? Change it up and go to a different teacher or a different studio. Are your headshots outdated? Get new ones. How's your footage on your casting profiles? Old and stale? Are you sitting around waiting for your reps to call you with an audition, or are you taking charge and creating your own projects? Do you have the type of job that will let you leave for an audition? Or are you getting too comfortable in your salaried position and don't want to mess it up, even though your dream is to act and you are miserable at this job? Well, do something!

How are you at auditioning? Safe? Be bold. Make stronger choices. What do you have to lose? Don't be middle of the road. Be *polarizing*. The worst feedback you can get is "He was fine. Nice guy. Showed up on time." Ew.

Don't. Just. Act. Stack your talent. Teach yourself how to edit. Take a cinematography class. Study other disciplines. Be ready for when that life-changing opportunity comes along, but don't obsess. Leave the door open for other avenues. Go out there and say yes to everything, meet people, get inspired, make art and make yourself more desirable.

You will be great because you will be the hardest working actor in the damn room. So be good to yourself, always be ready, don't be weird and please don't suck.

Love,
Matt

APPENDIX

<u>Casting websites</u>
NY Castings
Actors Access
Backstage
Casting Networks

<u>Podcasts</u>
That One Audition
Back to One
Off Camera with Sam Jones
Audrey Helps Actors
1 Broke Actress
Actor CEO
Meditation Oasis
Calm

<u>Books</u>
The Actor's Survival Guide by Jenna Fischer
Working Actor by David Dean Bottrell
The Science of On Camera Acting by Andrea Morris
The Charisma Myth by Olivia Fox Cabane
Acting as a Business by Brian O'Neil
Self-Management for Actors by Bonnie Gillespie
How to Stop Acting by Harold Guskin
The Present Actor by Marci Phillips

<u>Research</u>
CastingAbout
IMDBPro
Deadline
Hollywood Reporter
Variety
Bizparentz Foundation
SAG-AFTRA

Made in the USA
Coppell, TX
17 December 2021

69207946R00080